With Faith Like Hers Bible Study Series

I am Deborah

Carol Peterson, MTS

Honor Bound Books

Honor Bound Books

The *With Faith Like Hers* Bible study series and this book, *I am Deborah* is copyrighted by Carol Peterson, 2025.

All rights reserved. No portion of this book may be reproduced, stored in a retrieval system, or transmitted in any form or by any means—electronic, mechanical, photocopy, recording, scanning, or other—except for brief quotations in critical reviews or articles, without the prior written permission of the publisher.

All Scripture quotations, unless otherwise indicated, are taken from the Holy Bible, New International Version®, NIV®. Copyright ©1973, 1978, 1984, 2011 by Biblica, Inc.™ Used by permission of Zondervan. All rights reserved worldwide www.zondervan.com. The "NIV" and "New International Version" are trademarks registered in the United States Patent and Trademark Office by Biblica, Inc.™

Scripture quotations from the ESV® Bible (The Holy Bible, English Standard Version®), © 2001 by Crossway, a publishing ministry of Good News Publishers are used by permission of Crossway. All rights reserved.

Interior typeset in 12/16/18pt Cambria, used with permission from Microsoft. Cover background by Viscious-Speed; used with permission from Pixabay.com.

ISBN: 9781951587222

Dedication

This book is written with thanks to my terrific husband, Jim who has encouraged each of my writing projects with unwavering loyalty, and who patiently supported me going to seminary to better prepare for and follow God's leading in my writing.

This book is also dedicated to my daughter, Nicole and to every other woman as a reminder that they, like Deborah, have strength, wisdom, and fortitude to be warriors in their faith.

Contents

Preface

A Note about Deborah

Day 1 Becoming Like Deborah..1

I Speak for God

Day 2 I Wait on God...11
Day 3 I Speak God's Word..15
Day 4 I Trust in God's plan...19
Day 5 I Have Fire in My Eyes..23

I Have a Role in Judgment

Day 6 I am Wise...31
Day 7 I am Just...35
Day 8 I Do Not Judge Others' Righteousness....................................39
Day 9 I am Accountable to God...43

I am a Leader

Day 10 I Work to Serve Others..51
Day 11 I Face Difficulties...55
Day 12 I Provide Inspiration Through Action....................................59
Day 13 I Lead Others...63
Day 14 Others Watch for my Signal..67

I am a Warrior

Day 15 I am Courageous..73
Day 16 I Have Faith in Adversity.......................................77
Day 17 I Succeed Amid Odds..81
Day 18 I Support Those Wielding God's Power.....................87
Day 19 I Empower Others..91

I Live the Meaning of the Name Deborah

Day 20 I Know God's People are One................................97
Day 21 I am Hard Working and Persevere.........................101
Day 22 I Welcome Spiritual Transformation.......................105
Day 23 I Produce Abundant Fruit....................................109

I Sing the Song of Deborah

Day 24 March on, My Soul; Be strong..............................115
Day 25 I Recognize God's Cosmic Power..........................121
Day 26 I Praise God with Thanksgiving............................127
Day 27 I Sing of Redemption...131

Day 28 I am like Deborah…..………………………………...135

Resources……………………………………………………...143

From the Author……………………………………………...151

Preface

It is human nature to explore who we are. It is part of the spiritual journey we take as Christians to explore who we are *in Christ* and seek to understand who God wants us to become. This women's Bible study series focuses on understanding ourselves as Christian women.

I grew up in a Protestant Christian home. My father was a pastor so naturally I sat in the pew every Sunday and listened to his sermons. We also visited other churches whenever we went on vacation, where I heard sermons from other pastors, too. One thing I began to notice very early was the number of sermons that focused on men in the Bible. They were men of faith and had valuable lessons for us to learn. But as a young girl, growing into an impressionable young woman, I wondered what I had in common with all those "old dead guys," as I thought of them.

When I began writing this series about women in the Bible, I found that other women felt the same way. The lives of these women had been recorded in our holy Bible. They were there for an important reason; written and instructed by the Holy Spirit to be included within the canon of the church. After reading one of my books in this series, a woman commented that she had always felt as if she was not as loved by God as men were. She knew that was not true at an intellectual level, but she had never gotten over that feeling, until she read one of my books in this series.

My goal with this series is to address that issue; to point out how dearly God loves women by pointing out how clearly God loved the women whose lives He instructed the men who wrote our Scripture and recorded those lives in our Bible. Moreover, I wrote this series with the idea in mind that "we women are part of God's ongoing plan, just as were those women in Scripture."

Scripture gives us examples of people who lived by faith. They were people just like us—with flaws and foibles; triumphs and turmoil. But they lived a victorious life because they lived in the light of God's love. Outward things have changed since biblical times, but people are basically the same. When we look at the lives of women in Scripture, we glimpse how God saw them. When we learn the lessons they learned, God can show us how He still sees His women today. We can say, "I am like her; I have her faith; I can survive her circumstances."

That is the basis of the *With Faith Like Hers* series. Each book takes the reader through 28 days of meditative Bible study. We look at a woman in Scripture and see how God—through His Word—viewed her and how He might view our lives in a similar manner. This book is Deborah's story. But it is also ours—when we have faith like hers.

The book you are holding is *I am Deborah*. Since beginning to write the *With Faith Like Hers* series, God instructed me to go back to school. "Really?" I asked God in surprise. "You do know that I am almost 70 years old," I asked. Silence. But in ultimate obedience to that call, I completed seminary.

With my more secure understanding, I set out to revise this series of books. I was pleased (and more than relieved) to find that nothing in any of the books had been doctrinally incorrect. But I had more to say about each of these women. Sometimes a little; sometimes a lot. Thus, this book includes those power-packed initials after my name—MTS, referring to my Masters of Theological Studies. I add those little letters to give you one more speck of confidence that what I write is not something I whipped out of my back pocket. Contained in this book are lessons we can learn from the Old Testament prophetess and judge, based on sound doctrine from mainstream Christianity, studied and prayed over to encourage you, my precious reader, to live your life *with faith like hers.*

Although this book is intended to be an individual daily study, it can also be used effectively as a group study. Simply divide each weekly discussion at the sections—discuss one section each week. Add day 1 in with the first week; add day 28 in with the final week. Some weeks will have fewer days than others, but none will require more than one reading per day.

For ease of reading, I have limited footnotes within the body of the book. Citations for many of the resources I used for research are listed in an "annotated" Bibliography. I have added a few to this newest edition, thanks to serious study in seminary. "Annotated" just means that each resource includes a brief description of the value that resource held for me in the research of this book. Those descriptions can help you in your personal research, should you like to pursue this woman more deeply.

I pray you will be blessed in your study of Deborah and remember that your life—like hers—is part of God's ongoing plan.

A Note about Deborah

Deborah was an Old Testament prophetess and judge. As a judge, she ruled Israel after the nation had entered the Promised Land. She was one of Israel's rulers after Moses and Joshua and before Israel had kings.

For the next 28 days, we will look specifically at the life of Deborah. Each lesson will explore one character trait or circumstance of Deborah's life as recorded. Then we will examine: How can we live our lives like she did? How can our lives reflect what she has to teach us? How might God see us as His women of faith today in a way that reflects how He saw Deborah over 3,000 years ago?

What we know about Deborah is contained in two chapters in the book of Judges. Chapter 4 records the military campaign she led. Chapter 5, "Deborah's song," recounts that event in praise and recognition of who God is and what He has done. There is plenty we can glean from those two chapters.

This is Deborah's story. But when we learn the lessons taught us by this Jewish woman from ages past, we can say, ""I am like Deborah." I understand her life. I can live my life like she did." We can remember that our lives, like hers, are a continuation of God's ongoing plan.

Day 1—Becoming Like Deborah

☙❧

Many women in Scripture lived quiet lives of faith almost in the background. Even those women, such as Mary and Eve who played pivotal roles in God's plan, led quiet lives. But that wasn't Deborah's role. Not only did Deborah speak for God; she led the whole nation of Israel. And she led the Israelite army to victory over one of their fiercest enemies.

Let's look at who Deborah was and when and where she lived, to set the scene for our future lessons.

Background and When in History

The judges ruled Israel after the death of Joshua and before King Saul between 1360 and 1084 BC.[1] We don't know

---

[1] Ian M. Duguid, James M. Hamilton Jr., Jay Sklar, *ESV Expository Commentary.* (Wheaton, IL: Crossway, 2020), 512.

exactly when within that period of time Deborah reigned as some judges' rule may have overlapped or there may have been a period of time after the death of one judge and the time God "raised up" the next Judge.[2] We see that in the various times when Scripture tells us that people did evil in the sight of the LORD after the judge died (e.g., Judges 4:1).

Also Scripture references the time of the judges to be generally "after the death of Joshua" (Judges 1:1) with no indication of how long after Joshua's death God raised up the judges. But for our purposes, we can know that Deborah ruled after Joshua died and before the Israelite monarchy began. Her specific rule is recorded during the time after Othniel's and Ehud's rule, and before the rule of Gideon. Her story is recorded in chapters 4 and 5 of the book of Judges.

God raised up judges not only to rule the nation or settle disputes. He raised up people specifically to deliver His people from foreign oppression, to establish rest for the land, and to promote faithfulness by encouraging the people to keep their covenant with God.[3] That covenant included obedience to God's laws.

The office of judge was not dynastic. In other words, the position was not inherited, like the system of a monarchy where kingship was inherited by the king's child. Therefore, when a judge died, the people had to wait for God to raise up another person who would lead the nation.[4] The period of time after Joshua's rule and before the establishment of Israel's kingship was a reflection of the fact that the nation of Israel had rejected the Lord as their true King. We see that in Judges 17:6 which says

---

[2] Duguid, *ESV Commentary*, 516.
[3] Duguid, *ESV Commentary*, 512.
[4] Duguid, *ESV Commentary*, 516.

that "In those days Israel had no king; everyone did as they saw fit."

Some of those judges were good judges and led the nation well, such as the dagger-toting Ehud whose rule is summarized as good, reflecting the fact that his rule resulted in the land having 80 years of rest.[5] Other judges such as Abimelech, a tyrant who killed his 70 half-brothers, were not good judges and as a result the nation suffered and fell into sin. Other judges had mixed reviews, such as Samson, whose faith in God was rewarded with the presence of the Holy Spirit temporarily and with great strength, and who ended his life by using His God-given strength to take vengeance on his captors.[6] But Samson is most remembered for being duped by Delilah into revealing the source of his strength embodied in his hair.

The book of Judges records that twelve judges ruled Israel—six major judges (based on the amount of Scripture devoted to them) and six minor judges. Deborah is one of the major judges with two chapters in the book of Judges devoted to her. Of note, Ehud and Deborah are not described as having the Holy Spirit on them—even temporarily. Nevertheless, Bible scholars describe Deborah as an "exemplary" judge. [7]

In addition to being a judge, Deborah was also a prophetess. A prophet was a person who had the divine word, but was not necessarily associated with the Spirit. In other words, they spoke *for* God. Other judges talked *to God* or *about God*. Of all of the twelve judges who ruled Israel, only Deborah was God's mouthpiece. Only Deborah spoke for God.[8]

---

[5] Victor P. Hamilton, *Handbook on the Historical Books*, (Grand Rapids, MI: Baker Academic, 2001), 115.
[6] Hamilton, *Handbook*, 148-185.
[7] Hamilton, *Handbook*, 119.
[8] Ibid.

In addition to being a prophetess and judge, Deborah also led the Israelite army to victory over the Israelite's enemy the Canaanites, led by Sisera. Deborah was not a military strategist, nor does Scripture describe her as actively participating in battle. Rather, she led the Israelite army by being present, inspiring them, and assuring them that God was on their side in the battle. In this author's opinion, that battle presence qualifies Deborah to own the title, "warrior woman."

The Characters

In addition to Deborah, there are three other main characters in this account: Barak, Sisera, and Jael.

Barak was the person God chose to lead His people into battle. From a modern perspective, we might view Barak as a general over the Israelite army. God told Barak through Deborah to gather 10,000 men, assuring him of victory. Although Judges 5 indicates that other tribes participated in the battle, Barak is instructed to gather those men from Naphtali and Zebulun—two of the weakest tribes of Israel at that time.[9]

Sisera was the commander of the army of King Jabin, the king of Caanan. The Canaanites were Israel's long-time enemy. In the account of Deborah, we see that King Jabin had oppressed Israel for twenty years. It's important to note that Sisera and his army lived in the land of Canaan—the Promised Land and the very land which Israel occupied. In other words, the nation of Israel was being oppressed by its enemy from within its own land.

God had commanded Joshua and the Israelites to completely destroy the Canaanites before entering the Promised Land, so that His people would not sell themselves out.[10] Because Israel had not completely destroyed the Canaanites within the

---

[9] Duguid, *ESV Commentary*, 558.
[10] Duguid, *ESV Commentary*, 557.

Promised Land, the people had become influenced by them, resulting in a turning away from God. So God let His people be oppressed. Sisera was God's instrument of oppression. After 20 years of oppression, God showed grace toward His people, using Deborah and Barak to destroy the army and Sisera.

Jael was the wife of Heber. Heber was known to be a close ally of Sisera.[11] This is hinted at in Scripture when Heber had separated from his clan the Kenites who were descendants of Moses' father-in-law, ultimately moving his tent away from that clan.[12] Jael, however, did not evidently share her husband's feelings of alliance with Israel's oppressor. Rather, Jael is the person who proactively invited Sisera in to her tent where she provided a rug for warmth and milk to drink, before taking a tent peg and driving it into Sisera's temple.

In fact, when Deborah says that if she goes with Barak, then "a woman" would be credited for the victory, some Bible scholars suggest that the "woman" credited should actually be Jael; not Deborah, as it was Jael who personally killed Sisera.[13] While Deborah led the army, it was Jael who ultimately vanquished King Sisera. But notably, both women are remembered and credited for the victory.

Please read chapters 4 and 5 of the book of Judges as we study together. It's just two little chapters. You can read it all in one sitting; but take your time and enjoy the glory and depth. We start tomorrow, digging in and digging deep.

We modern gals can learn a lot from the character and circumstances of Esther. When we do, we get a glimpse of who we might be in God's eyes. Although this is Deborah's story, it is also ours, when we have faith like hers. At that point, we can say

"I am like Deborah."

---

[11] Hamilton, *Handbook*, 120.
[12] Duguid, *ESV Commentary*, 559.
[13] Hamilton, *Handbook*, 122.

For Thought and Discussion

- Who is the most memorable judge in your opinion? Is he or she remembered for being a good judge or a not-so-good judge?

- Explain in your own words the difference between a judge and a prophet.

- What did you learn about Deborah today that you didn't know before? How will that information influence you in this study?

PRAYER: Heavenly Father, thank you for Deborah's life and for including her story in our holy Bible. Please lead me through this study with an open heart and mind to learn lessons from Deborah and apply them to my life. Amen.

I Speak for God

Day 2— I Speak God's Truth

࿐

We modern folk hear the word *prophet* and think "old bearded guy in a long robe"—like Elijah and Isaiah as God speaks to and through him. Deborah was both judge, leading Israel in battle, and prophetess, receiving divine revelation. But more than just speaking God's truth, like other prophets, Deborah was God's mouthpiece. *She spoke for God.*

Deborah's job as prophetess was to receive messages directly from God and communicate them to the people. She was to provide moral and spiritual guidance. She was to call the people to repentance and warn people of the consequences of sin. She was to offer hope for restoration. She also interpreted God's law and His will, guiding people in their relationship with God.

Bible scholars debate whether or not God raised up any prophets after Jesus' birth. Certainly Jesus filled the job requirements of a prophet. He provided moral and spiritual guidance, called people to repentance, offered hope for restoration, and guided people in their relationship with God the Father, with Himself, and with the Holy Spirit. He was also God's mouthpiece—literally—as He was God Himself in human form. But Jesus was more than just a prophet.

Another biblical requirement for being a prophet was secondarily, sharing God's future plan. Many of the Old Testament prophets prophesied about Jesus' birth (e.g., Isaiah, Micah, Zecheriah) and the people's salvation through Him (e.g., Hosea, Joel, Daniel, Zechariah). Other Old Testament prophets prophesied about Jesus' second coming on the Day of the Lord (e.g., Joel, Amos, Isaiah, Zephaniah, Malachi, Jeremiah, Ezekiel).

We may not be able to provide that type of prophecy by relating God's revelation for the future. Nor are most of us being used by God as His mouthpiece—speaking *for* Him; speaking His words. But we can—and should—prophecy about God's plan for now. We can provide moral and spiritual guidance based on Scripture. We can call people to repentance based on Jesus' promises. We can warn people of the consequences of sin. We can offer hope for restoration. We can help others interpret God's law and His will gleaned from Scripture, guiding people in their relationship with Him.

And here's another thing. The presence of the Holy Spirit in people's lives in the Old Testament was rare. It was also often temporary. For example, King Saul received the Holy Spirit early in his reign, but then the Holy Spirit left him for good. When it came to judges, Othniel, Gideon, Jephthah, and Samson are said to have the Holy Spirit; not Deborah. As to prophets, Isaiah, Ezekiel, Daniel, and Zechariah are said to have the Holy Spirit; not Deborah.

We Christians today, however have received the presence of the Holy Spirit. When we allow the Holy Spirit to speak to and through us, in a way, we can be God's mouthpiece. We can speak God's truth, being careful to only share what we know to be true from Scripture, including how Jesus offers hope for restoration of a relationship with the Father. Like Deborah, we can be God's mouthpiece in a limited way—sharing the Gospel with others.

Who are we to God? When we recognize that we can speak God's truth, we understand how God might see His women of faith. We can respond:

"I am like Deborah."

For Thought and Discussion

- One of the spiritual gifts listed by Paul is prophecy (1 Corinthians 14:1-5; Romans 12:6; Ephesians 4:11). Who do you know who speaks God's truth to provide strength, encouragement, and comfort to others?

- With this definition of prophecy in mind, do you believe God has given you the spiritual gift of prophecy?

- How might you use Scripture in a way that provides strength, encouragement, or comfort to others? Who might you speak such prophecy to today?

PRAYER: Heavenly Father, thank you for your Word recorded in Scripture that strengthens, encourages, and comforts us. Help me share that strength, encouragement, and comfort with others in your name. Amen.

Day 3—I Wait on God

༂

It is hard to wait. Maybe we've made a wise and godly decision. Maybe the decision is even something we *want* to do to honor God. But sometimes we have to wait on God's timing. Well, of course we *have* to wait. But while we're waiting, God also wants us to have patience.

The other thing about waiting though is that God doesn't want us to just twiddle our thumbs or play 437 games of solitaire on our phone. He wants us to keep doing what we know we should do—living quiet lives of faith perhaps, until we sense that the time has come to act.

On the other hand, maybe God has said "Now!" and you're still waiting. You doubt His will or His answer to your question. Or you have stopped listening or trying to listen. What then?

Scripture tells us that the Holy Spirit will guide us (John 14:26; 16:13). We are to pray for guidance (Proverbs 3:5-6; James 1:5). And we are to keep doing the best we can until the Holy Spirit causes our direction to change.

I Wait on God

During that time of waiting, the LORD will renew our strength (Isaiah 50:31). Then those who love the Lord will go forth like the sun in its strength, knowing they can do all things through Christ, and remembering that the same Spirit who raised Jesus from the grave, lives in us (Romans 8:11; Ephesians 1:19-20).

Judges 5:28 records how Sisera's mother waited for him to return. She did not know God; had no faith or trust in Him. So all she could do—like others without God—was wait. Sisera's mother's waiting contrasted with Judges 5:31a which reminds us that those who love the Lord are like the sun when it rises in its strength. Sometimes God requires us to wait. Whether we wait or whether we do not have to wait, when the waiting is over, God wants us to move forward in His strength.

As God's mouthpiece, Deborah had patience in God's timing. All Israel had been under oppression for twenty years. They had been waiting in a sense, for God to act. Deborah knew the right moment to act to lead Barak to prepare for and enter the battle. She was steadfast and moved forward with God's strength. Deborah knew that waiting was not a time to be passive. Rather, waiting can be a time for patient, faithful preparation. It can also be a time of active discernment—being aware of what needs to be done, how to do it, how to prepare for it. She trusted in God's perfect timing and took decisive action at exactly the right time when He commanded it, telling Barak, "Go! This is the day in which the LORD has given Sisera into your hands" (Judges 4:14).

Who are we to God? When we recognize that we may have to wait on God's timing or instruction but then are expected to act, we understand how God might see His women of faith. We can respond:

"I am like Deborah."

I Wait on God

For Thought and Discussion

- Have you ever waited on God's timing? What was the situation? What was the result of waiting? Are you still waiting?

- What Scripture about waiting on God helps you during times of waiting?

- How does seeking guidance from the Holy Spirit help with the waiting? Or help you understand when the waiting is over?

I Wait on God

PRAYER: Heavenly Father, thank you for your patience with me but thank you also for nudges to act when I need them. Please help me be sensitive and obedient to your leading, Holy Spirit. And please help be remain steadfast during the waiting. Amen.

Day 4—I Trust in God's Plan

☙❧

If you had a friend who told you she would do something and didn't follow through, how hard would it be to trust her in the future? If you had a friend who always did what she promised, how likely would you be to trust her in the future? Trust is earned in human relations. It can also be broken.

Deborah's plans were rooted in confidence that God would deliver on what He told her. That confidence was based on thousands of years of history of God's relationship with the Jewish people. Many of the "songs" recorded in our Bible are recounting of that history. Hannah's song (1 Samuel 2:1-20) and Mary's song (Luke 1:46-55), for example recount that relationship. Other testimony from God's people recount it—Stephen's for example (Acts 7:1-53), and the many times the apostles repeated the history of the Jewish people as proof of God's trustworthiness. Many of King David's psalms sing of God's character of trustworthiness.

We'll look more closely at Deborah's song recorded in chapter 5 of Judges later, but for now, we recognize that Deborah trusted in God's plan. She knew that plan was good. So, she was able to live a life of righteousness, strength, wisdom, and courage because she trusted in Him.

We have that same recorded history that Deborah had—plus a few thousand years more of the history of God's faithfulness. It's that "cloud of witnesses" that Hebrews talked about (Hebrews 12:1). All those people whose lives were recorded in the Bible had faith in God based on what He had done—what He promised to do and then did.

Who are we to God? When we recognize that we can trust in God's plan and character and when we model our lives to be trustworthy in our own relationships with other people, we understand how God might see His women of faith. We can respond:

"I am like Deborah."

For Thought and Discussion

- Have you ever had a situation that caused you to question God's plan? How were you able to work through that? Are you still struggling? How might Hebrews' cloud of witnesses and the testimony of other Christian friends in your life help you?

- Is there a situation right now that requires you to trust in God's plan? Or do you know someone who is struggling to trust God? How might your personal experience or an event recorded in Scripture help?

- Do other people consider you to be trustworthy? Do you need to mend a relationship with someone based on broken trust, either yours or theirs?

PRAYER: Heavenly Father, thank you for your trustworthiness. Thank you that we know that what you say you will do, you will do, based on your character. Thank you especially for promising that our salvation is assured based on what you yourself accomplished, Jesus. Amen.

Day 5—I Have Fire in My Eyes

❧

One of the wonderful things about the much-loved TV show, *I Love Lucy*, was Lucille Ball's character. She got into trouble of her own making in each episode. She was smart and well meaning. But what made the show delightful was that she was feisty. She epitomized the stereotype of a "fiery redhead."

In the book of Revelation, the letter to the church at Laodicea (Revelation 3:14-22) condemned the believers for being lukewarm in their faith. To better understand what this comment meant to the audience at the time, we look at the geography of the area. Laodicea was one of three cities located in the Lycus River Valley. Laodicea, Colossae, and Hierapolis competed with each other for preeminence.

Hierapolis was known for its hot springs, believed to have healing properties. These hot springs made Hierapolis a popular travel destination. Colossae was known for its cold, fresh spring water which made it also a popular travel destination. Laodicea had neither hot nor cold springs. So the city of Laodicea built aqueducts to bring the hot water there from Hierapolis. By the time the water reached Laodicea, though it had become lukewarm. It was no longer soothing for bathing. Nor was it refreshing for drinking.

In Christ's letter to the church at Laodicea, He was not implying that He would rather have passionate pagans than ho-hum Christians. Rather, an understanding of the city's water reminds us of Jesus' claims that He was living water (John 4:10-14, 7:37-39). Thus Laodicea's water can relate symbolically to a person's faith. Faith can be both a source of healing relief as well as a refreshing encouragement to others. Underneath it all, though, Christ wants us to be passionate about our love for Him.

Put another way, Christ wants us to have fire in our eyes when it comes to our faith.

Let's talk Hebrew grammar. The Hebrew text in Judges 4:4 refers to Deborah as *eshet lappidot*. While this is often translated as "wife of Lappidoth," many scholars translate the phrase as "woman of torches" or "fiery woman." That interpretation is based on two translations. The Hebrew word *eshet* means woman in general, with a secondary meaning of wife. The Hebrew word *lappidot* is a feminine form of a word meaning *torch*. For that reason, some commentators interpret *lappidoth* as a description of Deborah as a *firebrand of a woman* or a fiery woman. I like to picture Deborah as a woman with fire in her eyes or "on fire" for God.[14] Here is a translation of this verse incorporating Hebrew words:

---

[14] Footnote for Judges 4:4 at Biblegateway.com accessed 9/3/25; Footnote referenced the Orthodox Jewish Bible (OJB) Copyright © 2002, 2003, 2008, 2010, 2011 by Artists for Israel International; Revised Geneva Translation (RGT) © 2019, 2024 by Five Talents Audio.

> *And isha Devorah, a neviah, the eshet Lapidot, judged Yisroel at that time.*

Thus the phrase *eshet lappidot* could be a description of Deborah's powerful and assertive nature. Deborah had fire in her eyes.

There is another person in Scripture who is described that way. Daniel 10:5-6 records Daniel's vision of a "man" dressed in fine linen, with a belt of fine gold. His body was like topaz, his face like lightning, his arms and legs like burnished bronze, **his eyes like flaming torches**, and the sound of his words like a great multitude. Bible scholars agree that Daniel's vision was messianic. The "man" was Jesus.

Did you notice? Daniel's vision reveals that Jesus had fire in His eyes. Jesus was focused on doing the will of the Father, with power and passion. If we are to model a life like His, we should have fire in our eyes, too. Like Deborah.

Who are we to God? When we recognize that God wants us to be passionate about Him, living a life on fire for Jesus, we understand how He might see His women of faith. We can respond:

"I am like Deborah."

For Thought and Discussion

- How does this explanation about the letter to the church at Laodicea make you think about your own faith? Is it easier for you to be healing to others or encouraging? Which might you need today?

- In what area of life do you have "fire in your eyes"? A cause? A role? For a person?

- How might you live your life of faith with fire in your eyes? What one thing might you do today to rekindle or ignite your passion for Jesus? How might you encourage other Christians to have a fire for Jesus?

PRAYER: Heavenly Father, thank you for Scripture that describes Deborah and Jesus as fiery. Help me model Deborah's faith in you today. Amen.

I Have a Role in Judgment

Day 6—I am Wise

❧❧

I don't know about you but I've made a whole lot of bad calls in my life. I've messed up completely many times. While Jesus has forgiven me of all of those unwise decisions, some of those bad decisions came with consequences. When we make bad decisions, sometimes those consequences change our lives and the lives of others forever.

Throughout the Old Testament, wisdom is praised. But not just wisdom in general. Rather, Scripture is clear that true wisdom comes from God. We have entire books of the Old Testament that deal with wisdom. In fact, Bible scholars divide the Bible into genres. One genre is referred to as the "Wisdom Books." Those books include Proverbs, Ecclesiastes, Job, and Psalms.

Solomon is often referred to as one of the wisest people in history (1 Kings 4:30-31). Solomon's first prayer recorded in Scripture was to ask God for wisdom in ruling the nation of Israel (1 Kings 3:9). And while he began his reign as king with wisdom, the recorded history of his later years note that he had 700 wives,

300 concubines, and made many less-than-wise decisions. As with all things, in wisdom, we must *continue* to rely on God for provision.

As a judge, Deborah was known for her wise counsel and sound decision-making. Deborah shows the critical importance of wisdom in guiding others. While all we know about Deborah is recorded in only two chapters of the book of Judges, there is never an indication that she ruled with anything but wisdom. Scripture freely records when otherwise respected leaders messed up even after a lifetime of wise living (e.g., King Saul, Lot's wife, Judas Iscariot).

Deborah's reputation as a wise leader, however remains honorable. In fact, some Bible scholars indicate that whereas all the other judges recorded in the book of Judges are declared dead at one point, there is no recording or statement of Deborah's death. Of course, she did die. But not recording her death is a subtle way to indicate the eternality of her reputation as a wise leader. It underscored the effectiveness of her rule.[15]

Who are we to God? When we recognize that we are to be wise and continue to seek and apply God's wisdom, we understand how God might see His women of faith. We can respond:

"I am like Deborah."

---

[15] Hamilton, *Handbook*, 120.

For Thought and Discussion

- What unwise decision do you wish you had not made in life? How has it impacted you over the years? What have you learned from that experience?

- What unwise decision that someone else made has affected you adversely? Have you been able to forgive that person? What lesson have you learned from that experience?

- What is one of the most important wise life lessons you know? How do you live it? How might you live it better?

I Am Wise

PRAYER: Heavenly Father, thank you for your wisdom. Forgive me when I rely on my own wisdom or worse, when I adhere to worldly wisdom that is not of you. Please help me always to seek your wisdom in all things. Amen.

Day 7—I am Just

❦

My mother-in-law often spouted wisdom. One piece of wisdom she often declared was, "Nobody ever said life was supposed to be fair."

Sometimes life isn't fair. And we moan and complain that it isn't. Sometimes we relish the fact that life isn't fair—when we're on the receiving side of the good stuff. We look the other way about how that unfairness is good for us but not so good for others.

Still, nobody ever said life was supposed to be fair.

While God is just, He isn't always fair. The fact is that we should rejoice in His unfairness.

Wait. What?

Through Jesus, the Father gives us mercy. We don't receive the punishment we deserve. That's not fair. Hallelujah!

Through Jesus, the Father gives us grace. We receive the blessings of forgiveness and salvation we don't deserve. That's not fair. Hallelujah!

I Am Just

The Father is just. He determined in His own wisdom and as part of His eternal plan that He would grant mercy and grace to all who believe in His son. Everyone who believes. That's *just* (justice) because He decreed it to be so. It's His decision, His plan. How He implements His plan is entirely up to Him.

But it's not fair from our human standpoint. We are getting what we don't deserve. Hallelujah!

> *Therefore the Lord waits to be gracious to you, and therefore he exalts himself to show mercy to you. For the Lord is a God of justice; blessed are all those who wait for him* (Isaiah 30:18 ESV).

That goes nicely with our earlier lesson about waiting for God. It can remind us to follow His example. We wait on God—His timing. He also waits to be gracious to us.

The Bible is filled with other verses about justice. Here's one I love:

> *But let justice roll down like waters, and righteousness like an ever-flowing stream* (Amos 5:24 ESV).

We often think of justice as harsh. We have to do what is right and if not—wham! Justice. But like wisdom, justice comes from God. God is just. He wants us to be like Him. That doesn't mean we must necessarily—or at least always—be harsh.

In Deborah's role as judge, she led the nation of Israel with justice. It was her job to uphold justice. She would have emphasized fairness and righteousness. She would have taught by example the importance of maintaining justice.

So should we.

And as we emphasize fairness and righteousness in our relationships with other people, we can continue to remember and rejoice that while God is just, His treatment of us as believers in His Son, isn't fair by human standards. Hallelujah!

Who are we to God? When we recognize that we are to uphold God's justice and treat other people justly, but also with a mindset of grace and mercy, we understand how God might see His women of faith. We can respond:

"I am like Deborah."

For Thought and Discussion

- Explain the difference between justice and fairness.

- We sometimes hear people say "how could God allow something like that?" Maybe you've said it yourself. Or perhaps someone has even said, "I can't believe in a God who would..." In what ways is that thinking an attempt to make God fit into a preconceived notion?

- What does it mean to you to treat others with justice along with grace and mercy? Is that something you struggle with?

PRAYER: Heavenly Father, thank you for being just. Thank you also for being gracious and merciful so that your treatment of those who believe in Jesus are treated unfairly from our human perspective—with your overabundance of grace and mercy we don't deserve. Amen.

Day 8—I Do Not Judge Others' Righteousness

❧❧

The older I get the less patient I am with people. I try to live by the philosophy that "everyone is just doing the best they can." Sure, maybe they could do better, or maybe at that point in their lives, they truly are doing their best. Either way, it is easier on my heart and mind to give folks the benefit of the doubt. As I age I have to spend a lot more energy reminding myself of that philosophy.

Christians are told two things about judging others. First, we are told not to judge people who are not Christians (1 Corinthians 5:12). That judgment is to be left to God because it is about their heart and about whether they truly know Him. In fact, we are not to judge the hearts of anyone as to their relationship with Him. Only God knows about that. We can leave that part of eternity up to Him. Whew!

That is not to say we do not have a responsibility to share what Scripture has to say about right living or to share the truth that morality comes not from what society has decided, but only from God. But in doing so, we are not to judge the eternal souls of other people.

Christians are, however, called to judge the *actions* of other Christians. No, we are not to stand them up on a stage and point out their every flaw in front of the world. Rather, we are to keep each other accountable to live what we believe. We are to do so gently and in a way that does not imply we are better than they are. We are to remind them of Jesus' teachings and that we are called to live a life modelled after His. We are called to keep other Christians accountable.

And other Christians are to keep us accountable in the same way.

God will take care of people's eternal judgment. Deborah judged only about legal matters in society. She based her judgment upon the law of Moses—given to God's chosen people by Him. Those laws assured justice and encouraged right living and right relationships between people and with Him. But even though she was God's mouthpiece, she would have left eternal judgment of people's souls to Him.

Who are we to God? When we recognize in what ways we are called to judge and also that we are to leave eternal judgment to God, we understand how God might see His women of faith. We can respond:

"I am like Deborah."

I Do Not Judge Others' Righteousness

For Thought and Discussion

- Explain the way we are to judge other Christians? How hard is it to judge other Christians based on non-essentials of salvation, such as the number of times communion is taken or the day of the week a person chooses to worship in a church setting? What has been your experience in those situations?

- How would you describe accountability between Christians? Do you have a Christian friend who is or who might be an accountability partner for you?

- What aspect of judging others do you struggle with?

I Do Not Judge Others' Righteousness

PRAYER: Heavenly Father, thank you that we do not have the responsibility or ability to judge the hearts of others but can trust in you to do so. Help me be accountable to other Christians and help me encourage other Christians' faith in a supportive way. Amen.

Day 9—I am Accountable to God

❧

I'm big on setting goals. Every December 17 (which happens to be our anniversary), Jim and I sit down and settle on things we want to accomplish in the following year. We categorize them by health, projects, travel, fun, and faith. But we don't stop at setting the goals. Every month in the following year, we meet again at our favorite restaurant, pull out the goals we set, and see how we did the previous month.

If we achieved the goal, we celebrate and usually set a new goal for that category. If we didn't achieve the goal we look at possible reasons why we didn't and importantly, we reaffirm the goal or set a revised goal for the next month. It's a form of accountability. It's one thing to say you want to accomplish something. It's another to have a plan to accomplish it and to be accountable for doing what you say you will do.

Scripture tells us that once forgiven, our sins are as far from the Father as the east is from the west (Psalm 103:2). Praise God! Hallelujah! Moreover, once forgiven, God doesn't even remember our sins (Jeremiah 31:34; Isaiah 43:25; Hebrews 8:12). More praising and hallelujah-ing!

Despite all that forgiveness, praising, and hallelujah-ing, Scripture also tells us that one day we will stand before the Father to give an accounting (Romans 14:12; 2 Corinthians 5:10; Matthew 12:36-37). Fortunately, the throne we will stand before is not about eternal judgment. That judgment throne is for unbelievers to be eternally judged (Revelation 20:11-15). God already knows our hearts. So we believers in Christ get to skip that judgment. Thanks to the personal testimony of the Holy Spirit living in us, the Father has already declared us His children, inheritors with Christ, forgiven and saved forever.

But we still have to stand before Him at the judgment seat of Christ and give an accounting. How did we do with the gift of salvation He gave us? How did we spend our time, energy, talents, and resources here in this one earthly life He gave us? Will He declare "well done, good and faithful servant" like Jesus suggested (Matthew 25:21-23)? Or will we despair over spending so many hours binge watching TV shows or wish we had spent more time serving the neighbor we knew was hurting? We will receive rewards (crowns given us for us to cast at Jesus' feet for our faithfulness) but also possible condemnation for things we did or did not do according to His will for our lives.

Our salvation is still secure. We still praise God for our salvation and for the satisfying works we do that honor Him. But also, ouch to think we may not be doing everything "as for the Lord." Or not using those gifts He gave us in a way that honors Him and brings Him glory.

As a leader of the nation of Israel, Deborah was answerable to both God and Israel. Israel was the nation of God's chosen people. Today, God's chosen people include us non-Jewish people who have accepted the Father's Son and who now have the

Holy Spirit living in us. Deborah knew she had been raised up by God for a specific purpose of guiding His people for a time.

Judges in the nation of Israel were considered to have been "raised up" by God for the purpose of ruling Israel. They were to rectify situations, utilizing God's grace in the judgments they made. God's grace was freely given. That grace at that time in history had nothing to do with the people's repentance. Rather, that grace had to do with an expression of God's character graciously extended to His people through His judges.[16]

God has also raised up each of us for a specific purpose. He has given us talents and spiritual gifts. He has given us resources. He has put us in specific locations and situations. He has placed various people in our lives. He has given us His holy presence, to guide and instruct us in life in each day and in each circumstance.

He has also called each of us to extend grace to others. Those people may not "deserve" our grace. We don't deserve God's grace either. Those people may not be interested in repentance. We might not have been interested in repentance at first either. Those people may not be ready to embrace the Gospel; worse, they may not be ready to even hear it. It took most of us more than one hearing to embrace it also. But God didn't give up on us. He asks us not to give up on others either.

Who are we to God? When we recognize that we are accountable to God for what we do and do not do here and when we use that recognition to help us focus on living a life that honors Him, we understand how God might see His women of faith. We can respond:

"I am like Deborah."

---

[16] Hamilton, *Handbook*, 111.

I Am Accountable to God

For Thought and Discussion

- Explain the difference between the eternal judgment of unbelievers and the judgment seat of God where we will stand for an accounting of how we lived our lives?

- Do you sense God leading you to do something big for Him with your life? Or something you might consider small, but might be big from His perspective? What is keeping you from starting?

- Explain the difference between working to "earn" God's love and salvation and using our God-given talents and gifts to pursue His kingdom plan out of love for Him. Which do you think would provide you with more personal satisfaction? Which do you think is of more value in God's view?

PRAYER: Heavenly Father, thank you that you have already looked into my heart and judged me to be yours eternally. Please remind me that I will also one day stand before you to give an accounting of what I did with the gifts, talents, and opportunities you have given me. Please help me live a life that honors you in everything I think, do, and say so that your response to me on that day will be "Well done, good and faithful servant!" Amen.

I am a Leader

Day 10—I Work to Serve Others

❧

Mother Terressa I am not! Here's where I'll confess something I'd just as soon keep private. There might be a need come up at church or in the community. I'm perfectly capable of pitching in. But my very first reaction is to wonder: how will this affect me personally?

Sigh. Ultimately I get there, jump in, and am glad I did, finding joy in the helping. But will there ever be a day when I don't first ask myself that self-absorbed and selfish question? It's one of those ways God is working to transform me. I am so grateful for His patience.

We picture Deborah sitting under her palm tree listening to people, making judgments, and settling disputes. She had that legal authority to administer justice and maintain order in society. That authority was given to her by God but was also recognized by the people of the nation.

As a wife, and perhaps a mother as would have been traditional for that time in history and society, Deborah surely had other duties. She might have had to keep her household in order, care for her husband and children. She may have kept a garden, made clothing for her family, tended the family sheep and goats. But she also had a distinguished career as leader of the nation of Israel.

Note that Deborah was a leader; not a politician. She hadn't been elected. She didn't have to answer to lobbyists or special interest groups. She simply had a reputation as an honorable leader, whose goal as leader was to serve others.

In Deborah's song (Judges chapter 5), she states that her heart is for the commanders of Israel who work willingly among the people (Judges 5:9). She didn't imply she was one of those commanders. She recognized their service and ended her praise for them with the statement "Bless the LORD!" Deborah served her people. She also recognized the service of others.

Jesus said He came to serve (Matthew 20:28). And He served in His leadership role, doing so with gentleness at times, but always with the full authority and power of the Father behind Him. If we model our lives like Christ, we too are called to serve others. And we can do so with gentleness and with the full authority and power of the Holy Spirit in us. One of Paul's most mind-boggling reminders is that we believers have the same power of the Holy Spirit living in us that raised Jesus from the grave (Romans 8:11; Ephesians 1:19-20). The same power—in the person of the Holy Spirit—who brought Jesus back to life, lives in us right now, today and every day. And we are called to use that power to serve others.

Who are we to God? When we recognize that we are called to serve others, whether in a position of leadership in our lives or not, and that we are empowered to do so by God Himself, we understand how God might see His women of faith. We can respond:

"I am like Deborah."

I Work to Serve Others

For Thought and Discussion

- Are you the first to volunteer or last to help fill a need? Do you actively look for what others might need? How do you proceed when you see something that needs to be done?

- Have you ever seen a need that seemed too overwhelming that whatever you might do was not enough? How did you proceed? Did you sense the Holy Spirit at work in the situation?

- What does it mean to you that even Jesus—God Himself—came to serve others? How does that help you model service in your life?

I Work to Serve Others

PRAYER: Heavenly Father, thank you that you modeled service to us through Jesus. Help me remember that even in leadership roles, I am called to serve others. Amen.

Day 11—I Face Difficulties

❧

Some days I hop out of bed and can't wait to get the day started. Other days, the hopping looks more like slithering, but at least I'm not at the "falling out of bed" stage yet. Inside my head and my heart, I'm still hopping, even on days that are difficult. Because you can't overcome difficulties by just staying in bed.

Deborah faced difficulties head on. At first, we picture Deborah holding court under the palm. It would be easy to imagine her lounging on pillows, beckoning parties to her to state their case. But each case presented to her was a difficulty to face. If the situations had been simple, the parties would not have had to come to her. But the people came. She faced their difficulties and made wise decisions on their behalf.

After only two verses of Deborah's story, a big problem comes up: it was time to go to war. We know that this big trouble wasn't something Deborah thought up on her own. She was God's mouthpiece, so she summoned Barak and asked him a rhetorical question: "Has not the Lord, the God of Israel, commanded you…" to gather an army against Sisera, the general of King Jabin's army?

I Face Difficulties

The problem had been growing for decades. When the Israelites crossed the Jordan River into the Promised Land, they were supposed to have killed all the Canaanites. A few however remained within the territory of the Israelites. By Deborah's time, King Jabin's general, Sisera, living in the Promised Land, had cruelly oppressed the people of Israel for twenty years (Judges 4:2-3).

Note that the reason God had allowed Sisera to oppress the people was because after the good Judge Ehud died, the people of Israel "did what was evil in the sight of the LORD" again (Judges 4:1). That continued the cycle of the history of the Jewish people from the time they entered the Promised Land, through the time of the judges and into the time of the kings of Israel and Judah. When a good judge or king ruled, the people prospered and did well. When a bad judge or king ruled, the people followed suit. The nation suffered and God allowed the people to be oppressed.

In Deborah's story, her rule of Israel began sometime after good judge Ehud died. The nation was in a mess again and the people were oppressed. Deborah wasn't surprised. The problem had been growing. The oppression had been going on for two decades. Then God determined that it was time to offer grace to His chosen people. Maybe they didn't deserve that grace, but He determined to rescue them anyway. So He gave Deborah the word: rescue the people.

Deborah didn't call together a group of advisors. Probably she prayed. But mostly what is recorded is that she acted. She faced difficulties head-on and remained steadfast.

I Face Difficulties

Who are we to God? When we recognize that we too can face difficulties head on and remain steadfast, we understand how God might see His women of faith. We can respond:

"I am like Deborah."

For Thought and Discussion

- Was there a time when you faced a difficulty that felt too overwhelming to deal with? Did you ignore it or take action? What was the result?

- What difficulty are you facing today? What big or small thing might you do to deal with that difficulty?

I Face Difficulties

- Is prayer the first or the last thing you resort to when faced with difficulty? How does prayer help? How does knowing the Holy Spirit is with you during difficulty give you peace?

PRAYER: Heavenly Father, we face difficulties in our lives. Help me never resort to blaming you for them. Help me always remember that you, Holy Spirit, are facing them with me and are ready to strengthen, comfort, encourage, and guide me through them. Amen.

Day 12—I Provide Inspiration Through Action

❧❦

We were standing at the edge of a cliff. Below was a lake. We had heard it was a deep lake. That was a good thing and a bad thing. Good that jumping meant we wouldn't hit a hard bottom; bad because the water was deep! So my friend jumped. I watched her fly through the air, slide through the water, and disappear. Then as she bobbed back up to the surface, a grin spread across her face. Sometimes we need inspiration through the action of others.

When Deborah summoned Barak, there is no record of any hemming and hawing. She gave Barak the order from God: gather your army at Mount Tabor. She would draw out Sisera and his army to meet Barak at the Kishon River. There Sisera's army would be conquered.

The only discussion that followed was Barak's remark that he wouldn't go unless Deborah went with him (Judges 4:8). So she agreed, simply replying that a woman—not Barak—would gain the glory of the battle. Scripture says: "Then Deborah arose and

I Provide Inspiration Through Action

went with Barak to Kadesh." After that, Barak gathered the troops and "Deborah went up with him" (Judges 4: 9-10). Deborah's bold steps inspired others to trust in God and act decisively, showing that leaders can motivate through example.

Who are we to God? When we recognize that we not only can be inspired by the action of others, we can also inspire others by the action we take, we understand how God might see His women of faith. We can respond:

"I am like Deborah."

For Thought and Discussion

- Was there a time when someone's action inspired you to do something you were afraid of, uncertain about, or not inclined to do? What was the result?

- Was there a time when you clearly inspired someone else by what you did? How did that make you feel?

I Provide Inspiration Through Action

- What action could you take to inspire someone else's deeper faith in Christ?

PRAYER: Heavenly Father, thank you for strong faith. Thank you for the inspiration of faithful people in Scripture and also of faithful people in my life today. Help me be a person who inspires others in a way that honors you. Amen.

Day 13—I Lead Others

☙❧

As Christians, we may or may not consider ourselves to be leaders. But all of us are leaders in some ways in our lives. As mothers or care givers or good neighbors, we often take the lead in helping or assisting others. Certainly, as prayer warriors, we can lead others in prayer.

Clearly Deborah was a leader. Deborah's role as a judge and leader of Israel demonstrates that leadership is not confined by gender. While Deborah lived within a male-dominated society, she broke traditional barriers with her authority and effectiveness. Similarly, service is not gender specific; we are all called to serve God and others. Sometimes leadership and service are combined, especially in roles we hold in our church.

Deborah was judge and prophetess. In our modern western society those titles are defined differently than they would have been for Deborah. Today, a judge sits in a courtroom and makes rulings based on law. While Deborah sat under a palm tree, she also made rulings based on Jewish law. The nation of Israel had no higher human authority at that time than that of judge. There was no president, prime minister, or king at that time. God alone was the higher authority and Deborah—as God's mouthpiece—was the person who ruled the nation of Israel based both on God's law and on God's instructions through her. She was the one person at that time who ruled the entire nation of Israel.

Imagine. Even in our modern society, it is rare for a woman to lead a country. Even then, a modern leader is subject to checks and balances from congress, courts, and people's opinions. Deborah however, ruled the nation of Israel alone under God's authority. And she did so with integrity and determination. She was a true leader.

Who are we to God? When we recognize that we are often called to leadership, and when we lead based on God's law and His guidance, we understand how God might see His women of faith. We can respond:

"I am like Deborah."

For Thought and Discussion

- What role of leadership do you hold in your life? What role of leadership might you hold in the future?

I Lead Others

- Do you have a role that includes both leadership and service? How do those capabilities work together?

- Who do you know who leads with exceptional integrity? How does that example influence your thinking about leadership and your own leadership skills?

PRAYER: Heavenly Father, thank you for placing me in situations which might result in leadership. Help me maintain integrity in those situations and remember Jesus' example of service in leadership. Amen.

Day 14—Others Watch for My Signal

൞൜

I was at a formal dinner party one evening. I had grown up with Emily Post and her rules of etiquette. I knew which fork to use for which food, where to place my napkin, and not to talk with my mouth full. But no one at that table picked up their forks or started to eat. Everyone was silent and still—waiting for the signal. Then the hostess sat down, picked up her fork, and took a bite of her food. That was the signal. The rest of us started eating, began to chat amiably, and enjoyed a wonderful evening.

Barak's army also waited for the signal. Ten thousand men followed Barak and Deborah to the battlefield. They faced Sisera and his army that included 900 iron chariots. But they waited. Then Deborah said to Barak, "Go! For this is the day in which the LORD has given Sisera into your hands" (Judges 4:14). That was the signal. Barak went down Mount Tabor with his men and defeated Sisera, his chariots, and his army.

Leadership isn't just about making decisions and telling people what to do. It isn't just about being an example by action. Sometimes, in that action, others are waiting for a signal. They are waiting to see what you will do. They are waiting for you to give the order. In that order should be an indication that what they are about to do will succeed or that it is worth the doing. Here, Deborah told Barak that he would win the battle. God had told her so and she relayed that information to Barak. That was the signal. It was time to begin God's battle and watch Him win.

As Christians, others are watching us to see if we live lives that reflect what we say we believe. We say we have compassion and generosity for others. Do we live with compassion and generosity? We say we forgive others. Do we? Or do we hang on to a grudge or judge others harshly? Other people are watching us. What signal are we sending out?

Who are we to God? When we recognize that others watch our signals and interpret their meaning as they relate to what we say we believe, we understand how God might see His women of faith. We can respond:

"I am like Deborah."

For Thought and Discussion

- What example of great leadership comes to mind? Did it include a signal to take action? How can you use that experience in your future leadership roles?

- How does an understanding that living a life of faith mean you are taking on a role of leadership so that others are watching to see how you live? How might you think about modeling your faith as "leading" others to Christ?

- In your leadership roles, do you include encouragement that what decisions you make or instructions you give will have an indication of success? How might you focus more on doing so?

PRAYER: Heavenly Father, thank you for the leading of the Holy Spirit in our lives. Remind me daily that your Spirit not only leads and empowers me, but is there to encourage me and also to remind me that there is a promise of success because the same power that raised Jesus from the grave is at work in and through me. Amen.

I am a Warrior

Day 15— I am Courageous

❦

In Judges 1 God commanded the tribe of Judah to battle the Canaanites. In Judges 4, Deborah delivered the word of God to Barak to battle the Canaanites. Deborah went with the Israelite army, standing with them. Although she was not a military strategist, Scripture says she led Sisera into Barak's hands. She was a warrior, a full participant in the battle as leader of the nation of Israel and she provided both inspiration and an example of faithfulness in the One to whom the battle belonged.[17]

I am afraid of goofy things—like the drain at the bottom of the swimming pool. That may sound goofy to others, but to me, those drains are scary. Maybe I've seen too many movies, but you just never know what might come up out of that drain. To stand before the troops—or even behind them on a battlefield—that would be super scary.

---

[17] Duguid, *ESV Commentary*, 557-558.

I Am Courageous

Throughout Scripture we see times when God's people were afraid. And throughout Scripture we read that God told His people—audibly or through someone else—not to be afraid. Joshua is one example. Three times God told Joshua to be strong and courageous; adding not to be afraid or discouraged. And the reason behind that instruction? Because "the LORD your God will be with you wherever you go" (Joshua 1:9).

Similarly Deuteronomy 31:6 commands God's people to be courageous—because the Lord goes with them and will never leave them. Psalm 46:1-2 reminds us that God is our refuge and strength so we will not fear even though the earth gives way.

Among the first thing nearly every angel who met up with a human being said was "do not be afraid!" (e.g., Genesis 21:17; Luke 1:13, 13, 2:10; Matthew 28:5). Because meeting up with a spiritual being can be scary. God recognizes that the spiritual world can frighten people. Thus, the angels sought to calm people.

Further, Paul reminds believers that they can have courage because they can do all things through Christ's strength (1 Corinthians 16:13; Philippians 4:13) and that of the Holy Spirit and that if God is for us, who can be against us? (Romans 8:31).

Life can be frightening. Situations can be daunting, especially amid uncertainty. Courage isn't a lack of fear. Courage is about doing what needs to be done even when you are afraid. Deborah fearlessly led Israel into battle against the Canaanites. She exemplified bravery in the face of challenge and danger. She knew God was on their side. So she was able to be courageous.

Who are we to God? When we recognize that we can have courage in life because God is with us, fights for us, and strengthens and empowers us, we understand how God might see His women of faith. We can respond:

"I am like Deborah."

For Thought and Discussion

- Do you have an irrational fear of something? Do other people think it's goofy? Why do you think you fear it?

- What fear do you have that is completely rational? How do you handle that fear? How has God's presence helped you handle that fear?

- Do you know someone struggling with fear? What might you say or do to help that person deal with that fear? What prayer might you pray with her?

I Am Courageous

PRAYER: Heavenly Father, sometimes I am afraid. Please remind me, Holy Spirit, that because you are with me I do not need to fear. Please give me words to en-courage someone else who is going through a frightening time. Amen.

Day 16—I Have Faith in Adversity

☙❧

Some days it's hard to even get out of bed. I didn't sleep well. I'm coming down with a cold; or coming out of one. I'm worried about everything or nothing. I'm too cold. Or too hot. Life is hard. The future looks bleak. Nothing is going my way. Everything is just bad.

And then I pray. And things look much better. Because I am reminded that God is in the situation with me.

One of the verses of Scripture that has changed my mornings is Matthew 6:33. There Jesus says, "seek first the kingdom of God and his righteousness, and all these things will be added to you." Those "things" point back to the previous verse from the Sermon on the Mount about worry over material needs. But Scripture also infers that seeking first the kingdom of God and his righteousness will also result in not worrying over anything else in life. That is echoed by Paul:

I Have Faith in Adversity

Do not be anxious about anything, but in every situation, by prayer and petition, with thanksgiving, present your requests to God. And the peace of God, which transcends all understanding, will guard your hearts and your minds in Christ Jesus (Philippians 4:6-7).

When I meditate on Jesus' instruction in Matthew, I like to take it literally. Seek the kingdom of God first—the very first thing to do in the very first part of the day is seek His kingdom. Pray. Read Scripture. Meditate. Ask for guidance, strength, help, comfort.

And God is good to provide.

Deborah was the ruler of her nation. That nation had been oppressed for twenty years. She knew Sisera would continue to oppress her nation until God did something. God did do something. He used Deborah to lead His people in tough circumstances. She had faith in God, His plan, and His ultimate victory over their oppressor.

Look at what she told Barak.

*"Go! This is the day the Lord **has given** Sisera into your hands. **Has** not the Lord **gone** ahead of you?"* (Judges 4:14, emphasis added).

Did you see that? Deborah relayed what God had told her, using past tense. God has already won the battle. The outcome is certain. A done deal in God's eyes. Therefore, it was a done deal in Deborah's eyes. And because it was a done deal in Deborah's eyes, it was also a done deal in Barak's eyes because he knew she spoke for God.

The reason for the certainty is because the Lord himself "went out" before Barak. In other words, the whole thing is a rhetorical question. Deborah wasn't asking Barak if the Lord had gone out ahead of him. She knew the answer. So did Barak. It was the Lord who was leading the battle. Deborah and Barak were just there among the troops. But like most of the battles in the Old Testament against God's enemies, the battle belonged to God. And if the battle belongs to God, He wins. Always. Done deal. Past tense, even if the physical battle hasn't yet begun.

The point for today is that Deborah faced adversity. But she had faith in what God would do and who He was. So too can we face adversity, with faith in what God wants to do in our lives, based on who He is and who we are to Him.

Who are we to God? When we recognize that we can have faith in adversity, we understand how God might see His women of faith. We can respond:

"I am like Deborah."

For Thought and Discussion

- What is the significance of the way Deborah used past tense to indicate what God was going to do (future tense)? How can we remember that whatever God promises is a done deal, even if it hasn't happened yet?

I Have Faith in Adversity

- What promises in Scripture do you hold on to during adversity that you consider a done deal—something God has promised that you can count on?

- In what area of this life do you recognize that God has gone before you? In what eternal area do you recognize that God has gone before you?

PRAYER: Heavenly Father, sometimes we forget that you created linear time only for our benefit. Thank you for Scripture that reminds us that what you have planned may not have occurred yet in our timeline, but that it has been accomplished because you are the one doing it. Amen.

Day 17—I Succeed Amid Odds

❦

Casinos make their money because the odds are in their favor. People flock to casinos because they think they—unlike everyone else in the casino—can beat the odds.

The Bible is filled with events where God's people beat the odds. But they only beat the human odds. The odds were never in favor of God's enemies. Only the house held the odds. That house belonged to God!

- Because if God is for us, who can be against us? (Romans 8:31).
- Because the battle belongs to the Lord (1 Samuel 17:47).
- Because "With man it is impossible, but not with God. For all things are possible with God. (Mark 10:27).

Gideon is a great example of beating human odds. God told Gideon (a good judge who lived after Deborah's time) to gather an army to fight the Midianites. Gideon initially enlisted 32,000 soldiers. But then God told Gideon he didn't need that many soldiers. So after two downsizing events, first to 10,000 men and then to only 300 men, Gideon faced the great Midianite army, along with the Amalekites, and other groups from the east "as thick as locusts" (Judges 7:12). In other words, Gideon faced overwhelming odds.

Gideon's army won. They succeeded despite overwhelming odds against them. But in fact, they had God on their side. Therefore the overwhelming odds were in fact against the Midianites, the Amalekites, and the "other groups from the east."

Similarly, 2 Chronicles records the battle between King Jehoshaphat and the army from Ammon and Moab. There Jahaziel told the assembly of Judah not to be dismayed at the "great horde" invading them, but to remember that the battle was not theirs but God's. All they needed to do was stand firm, hold their position, and watch what God would do (2 Chronicles 20:15-17).

It is for that purpose also that the author of Hebrews reminds his readers of the great cloud of witnesses. He recounts all the people who trusted in God and recognized the truth that the overwhelming odds in life were held by God (Hebrews 11).

In Deborah's story, the Israelite army consisted of 10,000 men from two of the lesser tribes of Israel. Sisera, on the other hand, had 900 iron chariots and troops described as a multitude.[18] Whatever number a "multitude" meant, it was more than Barak's army. This battle echoes King David's truth that, "Some trust in chariots and some in horses, but we trust in the name of the LORD our God" (Psalm 20:7; Isaiah 31:1).[19]

The issue of chariots and overwhelming military presence of the Canaanite army cannot be ignored. God had commanded Joshua to completely destroy the pagan nations when the

---

[18] Duguid, *ESV Commentary*, 558.
[19] Ibid.

Israelites entered the Promised Land. The first chapter of Judges details many of the battles and victories over Israel's enemies. Of significance however, is Judges 1:19 which records that the men of Judah took possession of the hill country, but were unable to drive the people from the plains, because those people had chariots fitted with iron.

Later, in Deborah's time, those iron chariots continued to present a seemingly insurmountable military power. But as the LORD did with Pharoah's army equipped with chariots when the Jewish people escaped from Egypt, God was able to deliver His people because of His own overwhelming might.[20]

Of interest, this military victory in Judges marks the last major effort by the Canaanites against Israel. David would later completely subdue the Canaanites. But Deborah's leadership in this battle against overwhelming odds marks the last time the Canaanites would dominate the people of Israel.[21]

Deborah would not have known the story of Gideon who became a judge after her death. Nor would she have known how King David slew the giant with a slingshot and faith in God. But she would have known about the Israelite people's escape from Pharoah's massive army equipped with chariots and horses. She would have heard about the battles Joshua had led as her people entered the Promised Land. She would have been familiar with Scripture that talked about the battle belonging to the LORD and that God led His people in battle. Those stories would have reinforced her and her people's understanding and faith that they could beat the overwhelming human odds because the true overwhelming odds were held by God alone.

Who are we to God? When we recognize that we are on God's side—the winning side in life, no matter the odds against

---

[20] Duguid, *ESV Commentary,* 557.
[21] Walter A. Elwell, *Baker Commentary on the Bible* (Grand Rapids, MI: Baker Books, 1989), 163.

I Succeed Amid Odds

us—we understand how God might see His women of faith. We can respond:

"I am like Deborah."

For Thought and Discussion

- How do reminders of the cloud of witnesses in Hebrews 11 encourage you? What other Bible stories remind us of the wisdom in trusting God?

- What challenge in life have you had to trust in God because the odds were overwhelmingly against you? Did you ultimately trust in God? What was the outcome?

I Succeed Amid Odds

- Is there a difficulty you or a loved one is now facing that feels like the odds are overwhelmingly against you? How can you recall Deborah's story and trust that God holds the overwhelming odds eternally?

PRAYER: Heavenly Father, it's hard not to look at situations from a human perspective and see such overwhelming odds against us. Please remind me that if you are involved then the odds are ever on your side and on the side of those who love you. Amen.

Day 18—I Support Those Wielding God's Power

❦

There are a lot of verses of Scripture where God encourages us to lead others. There are even more verses where God encourages us to follow Him. But there are also verses of Scripture where we are encouraged to follow other people who wield God's power. Deborah is an example of that.

In Judges 4:8, Barak agreed to go to battle against Sisera only if Deborah went with him. If she did not agree to go, he stated he would not go either. At first glance, it might sound as if he didn't have faith. But most Bible scholars disagree. Rather, Barak's statement is an expression of his dependence on God's word which God had entrusted to Deborah.[22]

Deborah didn't moan and complain about having to pack up and go with Barak. She didn't argue that leading an army wasn't in her job description. She just replied, "I will surely go

---

[22] Duguid, *ESV Commentary*, 558.

with you" (Judges 4:9). She knew what God had told her. She knew God would fight and win the battle. She also knew that her faith was stronger than Barak's because she had heard it straight from God whereas Barak was hearing it second hand. She recognized that the army needed a presence that would remind them in a clear and powerful way that God was on their side.

Deborah's story reminds us of Adam and Eve. Scripture tells us that God directed Adam not to eat from the tree of the knowledge of good and evil (Genesis 2:16-17). Most Bible scholars conclude that it was then Adam who relayed God's instruction to Eve not to eat the forbidden fruit. In other words, the instruction to Adam was clear because he heard it straight from God. Eve may have had a lesser faith in what God commanded because she only heard it from Adam. Of course, that means Eve *should* have gone back to Adam (or directly to God) for clarification after those instructions were called into question by the serpent. She didn't do that. But the point here is that a person who has clear instructions straight from God might have the stronger faith.

With Deborah, she had heard instructions straight from God. She also wielded God's power which He had entrusted to her as leader of the nation. It was natural and wise for Barak to request Deborah to go into battle with the Israelite army. Barak and the army supported those who wielded God's power. Likewise, Deborah who wielded God's power, supported the Israelite army, which was doing God's will.

Who are we to God? When we recognize that we are called to support those wielding God's power, we understand how God might see His women of faith. We can respond:

"I am like Deborah."

For Thought and Discussion

- How can we support people in ministry in our lives?

- Have you ever followed a charismatic leader only to discover that his leadership was not godly? Did his plan ultimately succeed or fail?

- How can you relate Barak's following Deborah's godly leadership to the disciples following Jesus? How does God's power make the difference in leadership?

I Support Those Who Wield God's Power

PRAYER: Heavenly Father, we recognize that you are all powerful, mighty God. We also recognize, Jesus, that you were granted all authority and power by the Father. We also recognize, Holy Spirit, the power you have in our lives. Please help me recognize that such power is available to me in my life and help me to wield it wisely in a way that honors you. Amen.

Day 19—I Empower Others

❧❧

As a young adult, I enrolled in a professional development program to build confidence and enhance my leadership skills. The 12-week course helped me be more effective in communicating and having more confidence in all areas of my life. Although it was not a Christian based program, it empowered me. Afterwards, I became an assistant in several courses for other students to help them learn what I had learned. I worked to empower others as others had empowered me.

Deborah encouraged and empowered Barak. Her role was judge and prophetess. She was not a military strategist, but she took a leadership role with the Israelite army in order to help Barak fulfill his role. Deborah shows us how effective leaders lift up those around them. They mentor, encourage, and empower others under their leadership to succeed.

We also are called to mentor, encourage, and empower others in their faith. Paul was great at that. He told people to have patience and grace for others who might not be as strong in their faith (Romans 14:1-4). Similarly we are called to keep each other accountable and share our understanding of God's plan with others, including other Christians, as "iron sharpens iron" (Proverbs 27:17).

Deborah's actions and her sharing God's word empowered Barak individually. They also empowered the Israelite army. Who are we to God? When we recognize that we are to encourage, empower, and mentor others, we understand how God might see His women of faith. We can respond:

"I am like Deborah."

For Thought and Discussion

- Have you ever said or done something in order to empower someone else to do something difficult? Have you ever empowered someone through your example?

- Who has mentored you in your faith? How did they do that? What specific things did they say or do to encourage, empower, or mentor you?

- Who might God be leading you to mentor in their faith? What one thing might you do today to encourage that person?

PRAYER: Heavenly Father, thank you for placing people in my life to encourage, empower, and mentor my faith. Please help me be one of those people for someone else. Amen.

I Live the Meaning of the Name Deborah

Day 20—I Know God's People are One

☙❧

I love that names have meaning. I often pray that people I know will live the meaning of their names. My name, Carol, means "joyful song." Despite that meaning, I am sometimes grumpy. On those days, I pray especially hard to live the meaning of my name, not only to encourage my own joyfulness, but also to be a joyful song to others.

The name Deborah means "bee." Yes, bee, like the little black and yellow striped insect. How in the world could a person live the meaning of "bee"? Moreover, why would a person want to?

Bees have symbolized many things throughout the centuries and among different cultures. And except for getting stung by bees, all of the things bees symbolize are good. So we'll look at a few of them.

Today we recognize that bees are known for their social structure and teamwork within hives. In the hive, there is a queen bee who is generally in charge. All of the other bees are "worker bees," who do her bidding. Let's focus on the community aspect.

Because of their social structure, bees symbolizes the importance of community and cooperation in human society. God created people for relationship—husbands and wives, friends, our relationship with God. God wants us to have good relationships, especially our relationships with other Christians.

The importance of unity of God's people is repeated throughout Scripture. We are to focus on our relationship with God first. In the Old Testament, the question is repeated, "Who is on the LORD's side?" (Exodus 32:26).[23] In the New Testament, Jesus repeatedly says "Come to me" (Matthew 11:28-29), referring to the importance of our relationship with God.

We are also to focus on our relationship with other believers. In the Old Testament, many of the 613 laws in the books of Genesis, Exodus, Leviticus, Numbers, and Deuteronomy set out instructions for God's people to live together in community and harmony. In the New Testament, most of the Apostle Paul's letters command the early church members to have unity (e.g., 1 Corinthians 1:10; Ephesians 4:1-3; Philippians 1:27).

Simply put, our lives are better if we live in community with God and with each other. Bees are great examples of living in community. They live together and they work together in cooperation, building their hive and sweetening the world with what they create.

Who are we to God? When we recognize that God wants us to live lives of community and cooperation, we understand how God might see His women of faith. We can respond:

"I am like Deborah."

---

[23] Duguid, *ESV Commentary*, 563.

For Thought and Discussion

- What is the best example of teamwork you have experienced? Was it within the church or in secular society?

- Is there an area in your church that works together especially well? Is there an area of division? How do you sense God wanting there to be unity?

- Do you know the meaning of your name? If not, consider doing a search online to discover the meaning. How might you pray that God would help you live the meaning of your name?

I Know God's People Are One

PRAYER: Heavenly Father, thank you for creating people to live in community with you and with each other. Please show me areas of my life where there needs to be more unity. Please lead me to help promote unity in every situation. Amen.

Day 21—I am Hard Working and Persevere

❦

When I'm busy, I feel good. Admittedly, sometimes I also feel tired. Even worn out. But when I'm not busy, when I'm sitting around or doing something half-heartedly, I feel sluggish and distracted. And sometimes worthless. Ugh!

The industrious nature of bees reflects hard work and perseverance. The Apostle Paul talks a lot about hard work and about perseverance in faith. We can't imagine a more hard working person than Paul. He traveled throughout the middle eastern world and up into Europe establishing churches. He returned to visit many of those churches, writing extensively to further instruct the church members in theology and how to live a life that reflects their faith.

Everywhere he went, Paul preached and taught and worked at jobs to help support himself and the church. He was beaten, imprisoned, persecuted, and killed for his faith, but he never gave up. And through it all, he wrote about his own journey of faith and the importance of persevering through trials to reach the goal—Heaven.

I am Hard Working and Persevere

Remember clearly that we are saved by what Jesus did. We can never do anything on our own to earn our salvation. We are not saved by our "works." But, once saved, God wants us to live out our faith in gratitude for what He did for us. He gifted us with talents and abilities and expects us to use those gifts to raise up, encourage, and empower His church. Ephesians 2:10 acknowledges that we are God's handiwork created in Christ Jesus *to do good works, which God prepared in advance for us to do*. Works are not about salvation. Works are about being a part of God's plan and pursuing our specific purpose within that plan.

Remember Day 9 and the discussion of being accountable to God for our faith and the work we did in this life? If God were to judge the bees, I'll bet he would tell each one of them, "well done, good and faithful servant!"

One meaning of the name Deborah is about being hard working and persevering. Deborah worked hard, judging, speaking God's word, and leading the army into battle. She also persevered in her faith. She lived the meaning of her name, showing those characteristics of hard working bees.

Who are we to God? When we recognize that God wants us to work hard for Him and persevere in our faith, we understand how God might see His women of faith. We can respond:

"I am like Deborah."

For Thought and Discussion

- In what way do you sense God is leading you to work hard for His kingdom? What gifts and talents has He given you for that task?

- How have you struggled to persevere in your faith? What has helped you? What could help you further?

- Who in your life needs encouragement either to use their gifts and talents for the kingdom or to persevere in their faith? What can you do today to encourage that person?

I am Hard Working and Persevere

PRAYER: Heavenly Father, thank you for your creation. Thank you for the industrious bees who can exemplify ways to live our lives in ways that honor you. Please help me work hard and persevere in my faith in you. Amen.

Day 22—I Welcome Spiritual Transformation

ೞ✿ೞ

I regularly pray a particularly scary prayer. "Please keep changing me into the woman you desire me to be." That's scary because it recognizes that I'm not there; there is more God wants me to be, maybe something completely different from who I am right now. And although I can look back and recognize how my faith has grown, what life lessons I have learned, and what wisdom I have gained, I also recognize that God is so great in His plan for even little me, that what He envisions for me is something I probably have no concept about. It's about surrender to His will. Fortunately, that surrender is in recognition that whatever He has in mind for me is better than anything I could come up with on my own. Still, the unknown can feel scary.

So what does that have to do with bees? Biologically, the life cycle of bees goes from egg to larva to adult insect. Many cultures therefore see that bees symbolize transformation and personal growth. This can represent the potential for change in individual people.

I Welcome Spiritual Transformation

The only facts we know about Deborah come from Judges chapters 4 and 5. We don't know the path her spiritual journey took her. But we can infer that she probably didn't have unusual wisdom at age three. Nor did she probably hear God speak commands to her as a child. She likely went through her own spiritual transformation as she was receptive to God's leading and open to what He had in mind for her life. Then she eagerly joined His team, set up shop under the palm of Deborah, and became His mouthpiece.

Deborah lived the meaning of her name. Like bees, she was open to how God could transform her spiritually and use her for His great, big purpose.

Who are we to God? When we recognize that God is at work transforming us into the women He desires us to be and when we are open to that change, we understand how God might see His women of faith. We can respond:

"I am like Deborah."

For Thought and Discussion

- Summarize your journey of faith up to this point in three sentences. What was your life like before Jesus? What were the circumstances when you met Jesus? How is your life different today? This is your testimony.

I Welcome Spiritual Transformation

- What life struggles consumed you before you met Jesus? How has knowing Jesus helped you deal with those struggles? What prayer might you pray to help you deal with those struggles more effectively?

- Imagine yourself in ten years. How do you imagine your faith has grown? How has God transformed you?

PRAYER: Heavenly Father, thank you for loving me enough to want me to become the very best version of me. Thank you for continuing to transform me spiritually and for having patience as I sometimes hesitate or resist that transformation. Remind me that your vision for who you want me to become is better than anything I might imagine on my own. Amen.

Day 23—I Produce Abundant Fruit

❦

I *love* baklava! Miniature triangles of flaky pastry layered with crushed pecans and drizzled with honey. Yum!

As bees flit from plant to plant, they spread pollen. That process is essential for plant reproduction. Drive through a farmland and count the little white boxes piled up in the fields. Those boxes are homes for thousands of bees, placed there by farmers to aid in food production in those fields.

Plus, bees produce piles of sweet and delicious honey that delights our taste buds. Archaeologists have found honey stashed inside jars and placed within Egyptian tombs. Thousands of years later, the honey is still edible. Honey is imperishable. So is the Gospel. So is the endurance of our faith.

Deborah lived a life that produced spiritual fruit. God gave Deborah the spiritual gifts of wisdom and prophecy. She used those spiritual gifts to lead the nation of Israel to have better community and cooperation among citizens in settling their disputes. She used those spiritual gifts to lead the nation of Israel out of oppression from their enemy.

I Produce Abundant Fruit

Depending on which Bible scholar you follow, the Bible lists anywhere from a dozen to 26 spiritual gifts. You can create your own list of those gifts, by going to 1 Corinthians 12:1-31, Romans 12:6-8, and 1 Peter 4:9. Some gifts might overlap or you might interpret Scripture to list a gift other people might not see. Here is the list I see in Scripture:

Wisdom
Knowledge
Faith
Healing
Miracles
Prophecy
Discernment
Speaking in Tongues
Interpretation of Tongues
Service
Exhortation
Leadership
Service
Giving
Administration
Evangelism
Discipleship
Teaching
Encouragement
Apostleship (establishing and leading churches)
Hospitality

God has not given everyone all of these spiritual gifts. And maybe the Holy Spirit has not yet revealed gifts He wants us to use in the future. But you can be sure that if you are part of God's family, you have received spiritual gifts. And God wants—even expects—you to use them to honor Him and build up His church. Remember Ephesians 2:10?

> *For we are God's handiwork, created in Christ Jesus to do good works, which God prepared in advance for us to do.*

The meaning of Deborah's name reminds us that, like the industrious bee, God intends us to use our spiritual gifts and produce abundant spiritual fruit. Deborah's life exemplified that meaning also. She used her spiritual gifts and led the nation of Israel producing spiritual fruit of following God's lead out of oppression and toward redemption.

Who are we to God? When we recognize that God has given us spiritual gifts and expects us to use them to produce spiritual fruit which benefits others and brings honor to Him, we understand how God might see His women of faith. We can respond:

"I am like Deborah."

For Thought and Discussion

- Who do you know who clearly exhibits some of those listed spiritual gifts? How do those people use them for God's kingdom?

I Produce Abundant Fruit

- Do you know what spiritual gifts God has gifted you with? What are they? If you don't know, can you locate an online test to find out what they are?

- How do you sense God leading you to use your spiritual gifts? What first step can you take to use them?

PRAYER: Heavenly Father, thank you for the spiritual gifts you have given me. I ask you to make clear to me which spiritual gifts you have blessed me with. Please then lead me to use them appropriately and for your glory. Amen.

I Sing the Song of Deborah

Judges Chapter 5

Day 24—March on, My soul; Be Strong!

☙❧

I didn't make it as cheerleader. But I was on the drill team. Boy, could we march around during halftime! We were, in fact, very awesome!

Judges chapter five is labeled "The Song of Deborah" in our Holy Bible. Bible scholars break the song down into sections so we can better understand what Deborah is relating and what it means. Here is one such breakdown:[24]

- Introductory thanksgiving hymn (Judges 5:2-11d). This section calls the people to hear the praise that follows. Yahweh is declared to be the source of Israel's help. Then there is a description of Israel's oppression and a call to celebrate God.

---

[24] Hamilton, *Handbook*, 124-127.

- The next section records the summoning of the tribes of Israel to join the battle and the naming of the participating tribes (Judges 5:11e-18). There is censure of four tribes which did not participate. There is special honor for two tribes.

- The final section describes the battle and the aftermath (Judges 5:19-31), including the account of Jael killing Sisera, the taunting of Sisera's mother, and the conclusion of the song invoking Yahweh's blessing.

For today we will look at Judges Chapter 5:21—"March on strongly, my soul." This focus is part of the battle section of the song. It reminds us of the good old hymn, *Onward Christian Soldiers*" (Lyrics by S. Baring-Gould; music by St. Gertrude, 1865). This great hymn reminds us that we are "marching as to war" against Satan. It reminds us that, "Like a mighty army moves the church of God."

That song itself reminds us of the Salvation Army. The Salvation Army isn't just a group of bell ringers at Christmas, a chain of thrift stores, or a place where homeless people can get a hot meal. The Salvation Army is a Protestant denomination within the evangelical movement. As part of their faith, members agree to "the Soldier's Covenant," which is a simple creed similar to most mainstream Christian denominations. It includes belief in the Trinity, salvation through grace, and the importance of sharing the Gospel. Members are referred to as "soldiers of Christ." I'm not suggesting anyone switch denominations. I mention this international Christian denomination to point out their recognition of the clear military theme presented throughout the Bible.

Even in the New Testament.

March On, My Soul; Be Strong!

It's easy to see the battles throughout the thousands of years of history recorded in the Old Testament. But a strong military theme also exists in the New Testament. Many of Paul's letters incorporate a military motif. He calls Timothy his fellow soldier in Christ (2 Timothy 2:3-4). Paul refers to himself as a prisoner of war, or prisoner for Christ (Ephesians 3:1; Philippians 1:1). He tells Christians to put on the armor of God (Ephesians 6:10-18) because there is a spiritual battle and we are called to stand firm and fight against the evil one.

But another old hymn also comes to mind today. "It is Well With My Soul" (Lyrics Horatio G. Spafford, 1873; music by Ville du Havre, 1876). This hymn is filled with truth. Everything in life, and especially our relationship with God is well with our soul, because of Jesus. Furthering the military theme and fight against Satan, this hymn says, "Though Satan should buffet, though trials should come," ... whatever else...it is well with my soul."

Because it is well with our soul and because we have strength that comes through Christ and because we are empowered by the Holy Spirit in us, we can march on. Like Deborah, we are God's warrior women!

Who are we to God? When we recognize that we are called to participate in God's battle over evil, we understand how God might see His women of faith. We can respond:

"I am like Deborah."

March On, My Soul; Be Strong!

For Thought and Discussion

- We see a lot of battles in the Old Testament section of our Bible. But the battle theme continues in the New Testament as well. What military aspect in the New Testament comes to mind?

- Have you ever considered yourself to be a soldier fighting evil in God's army, which is the church? How might that understanding influence how you live your life?

- How does the military theme of Scripture complement God's overall plan of redemption?

PRAYER: Heavenly Father, thank you that the battle belongs to you. Thank you for assuring us that you have already won the battle against evil. Please strengthen and encourage us as we stand firm and fight evil as your warrior women! Amen.

Day 25—I Recognize God's Cosmic Power

֍

Some people see science and faith as contradictory. I prefer to think of science as mankind's way of trying to understand God's plan for the universe. Science often gets things wrong (the world is flat; the sun revolves around the earth; we know all there is to know of the universe). But nonetheless, science keeps trying to understand God's plan. I even think it can be honoring to God that we are trying to understand His plan—as long as we are not denying His existence in the process!

The scientific theory of the decaying universe (sometimes called cosmic decay) is based on the decline of the universe leading to its ultimate end. Not surprisingly to Christians, that theory of cosmic decay generally coincides with God's plan revealed in Scripture. One day this earth will cease to exist. That's where science ends though and faith continues. Scripture tells us that at the end of days, God will then create a New Heaven and a New Earth. That truth is revealed throughout both the Old and New Testaments, referred to variably as the day of the Lord,

I Recognize God's Cosmic Power

judgment day, the day of reckoning, and the end times, culminating in the book of Revelation describing Jesus' return.

The point for today is that throughout everything and throughout all time, God alone is in charge of the cosmos.

Judges 5:4-5 highlights the cosmic power of God to fight from Heaven for his people (Judges 5:20-21).[25] In Judges 5:20, attending the Lord in battle were His heavenly forces, called "the stars" of heaven.[26] The reminder in Judges 5:31a that one day all of God's enemies will be destroyed and cast out, takes us to that same scene in Revelation 19:11-21.[27] These verses remind us that the God who delivered His people from Egypt with great cosmic signs and judgments is the same God who delivered His people during Deborah's time and continues to save, deliver, and provide for his people today.[28] And He will do so in the future, even to the point of creating a New Heaven and a New Earth.

Let's follow the scene of the battle. Judges 5:4 states that God had caused the heavens to pour down water during the battle with the Canaanites. As a result, the River Kishon had suddenly flooded the plain. That flood caused Sisera's army to be swept away (5:21) and his chariots to be ineffective. Sisera himself had to leave the safety of his chariot and flee on foot (4:15), likely due to the impassibility of the mud caused by the heavy rain or by the flood itself.[29] As one Bible scholar explains, "the entire natural world seemed to conspire to assist Israel."[30]

That display of God's power in nature reminds us of God's display in Exodus 14, where He caused the sea to open allowing

---

[25] Duguid, *ESV Commentary*, 562.
[26] Duguid, *ESV Commentary*, 564.
[27] Duguid, *ESV Commentary*, 565.
[28] Ibid.
[29] Duguid, *ESV Commentary*, 560.
[30] George Arthur Butterick, Commentary Editor. *Interpreter's Bible* (New York: Abingdon Press, 1952), 717-718.

Israel to pass through but then closing in on their enemy, defeating them with water.[31] It was also a reminder that when God is involved, what once was a military advantage (the chariots) can become a liability.[32]

This section of Deborah's song reminds us that God controls the cosmos. More than that, the cosmos can become His weapon to fight for His people and to battle evil in the world. One day the cosmos He created will end, but praise God, He will create a new and better Heaven and earth for His people and all of creation. Deborah experienced God's power and control of the cosmos first hand.

Who are we to God? When we recognize that we are part of God's creation and that He is in control of the cosmos, we understand how God might see His women of faith. We can respond:

"I am like Deborah."

---

[31] Duguid, *ESV Commentary*, 562.
[32] Hamilton, *Handbook*, 562.

I Recognize God's Cosmic Power

For Thought and Discussion

- What part of God's creation fills you with joy? Nature here on earth? The vastness of the universe? Microscopic life so small we are not even aware of its existence?

- Does the end of days fill you with fear or hope? How does the idea of an end to the creation that now exists affect your thinking about stewardship?

- What other verses of Scripture come to mind about God using nature to fight battles or overcome evil forces?

PRAYER: Heavenly Father, thank you for the natural world and also for the heavenly realms. Thank you that you are in control of it all. Help me see your power in nature and the cosmos today as a reflection of your character and plan for your world. Amen.

Day 26—I Praise God with Thanksgiving

☙❧

Philippians 4:6-7 commands us to pray in all circumstances and to do so with thanksgiving. It's easy to pray with thanksgiving when things are good. It's harder to do so when circumstances are challenging; more so when things are dire.

The first time I used Paul's prayer "technique," was when my dear mother-in-law was dying. I was deeply blessed to be with her that week to help in her care. She had terminal cancer—the last episode of cancer after 40 years facing cancers of various types. There was no cure this time; nothing that could be surgically removed. No radiation, chemotherapy, immunotherapy, or natural treatments would help; much less cure her. She was no longer able to speak but there was still weak evidence that she was aware of her surroundings. So I prayed over her. With thanksgiving.

I prayed with thanksgiving for her life. For her children. For my children who came through her son. For her example of living. For the joy she brought to others in general, and to her family and to me personally. I prayed with thanksgiving for her legacy of faith.

As I said "amen," I opened my eyes. Rosemary was gazing at me through tears. She knew she was dying. She had no hope of continued life on this earth. But her tears were tears of gratitude; tears of thanksgiving for her own life and for the very same things I had prayed for in thanksgiving, asking God to give her comfort and strength and to give her family comfort and strength as well—based on our faith in the One from whom all blessings flow.

Deborah's song includes praising God with thanksgiving. Judges 5:2-3 is a call to worship beginning with the words, "Bless the LORD!" Then Deborah gives God credit for His deliverance, remembering the wondrous things the Lord has done for his people (e.g., Psalm 119:18). Thus this reminder was her God-led remedy to counter the idolatry of forgetting.[33] As one Bible scholar says,

> *The account of Deborah and Barak provides assurance that the Lord is gracious to his people and sustains them, as he rehearses the patterns of redemption over and over again across the pages of Scripture.*[34]

Moreover, Deborah's song is an example of what our own prayer life could be. We call ourselves to first worship Him. We recount what He has done for us, remembering that He is gracious and sustains us in all things. Throughout Scripture, we are called to remember God—who He is, what He has done, and what He has promised to do (e.g., Deuteronomy 8:2; Ecclesiastes 12:1; Isaiah 46:9; Psalm 119:5; John 14:26). The sacrament of Holy Communion (also called the Eucharist and the Lord's Supper)

---

[33] Duguid, *ESV Commentary*, 562.
[34] Duguid, *ESV Commentary*, 566.

I Praise God with Thanksgiving

itself is meant to be a reminder of divine Christ—who He is, what He did for us, and what He has promised to do. Deborah reminds us to remember God and to do so with thanksgiving.

Who are we to God? When we recognize that we should praise God in all circumstances, remembering who God is, what He has done, and what He has promised to do, we understand how God might see His women of faith. We can respond:

"I am like Deborah."

For Thought and Discussion

- What blessings do you regularly praise God for with thanksgiving?

- What things in your life do you struggle to praise God for with thanksgiving? How might you seek to find one blessing amid the struggle to praise Him for, even if it is "only" that the Holy Spirit is going through it with you?

I Praise God with Thanksgiving

- What things do you struggle to remember about God? What things might you seek to remember with praise and thanksgiving?

PRAYER: Heavenly Father, I praise you for who you are, what you have done, and what you have promised to do. Help me praise you more. Amen.

Day 27—I Sing of Redemption

☙❧

Christians bandy certain theological words about almost willy-nilly; often without really understanding what they mean or what they are based on. "Redemption" is one of those Christianese words we hear in church but aren't always sure about its exact meaning. The theological concept of redemption is based on legality. It is a matter of buying back or paying for the person redeemed.

In the Old Testament the object of God's redemption was almost always His people as a whole, as the entire nation of Israel. In Deborah's situation, God redeemed (freed) His people from oppression from the Canaanites. In that instance, God did not pay for that redemption, He did so by His power.

> "I am the Lord, and I will bring you out from under the yoke of the Egyptians. I will free you from being slaves to them, and I will redeem you with an outstretched arm and with mighty acts of judgment" (Exodus 6:6).

I Sing of Redemption

In the New Testament, God also redeemed His people by His power. But in the New Testament, He did so by paying a price for that redemption, not only of His people as a group but also for His people individually. He paid that price *to Himself* and *by Himself* through the sacrifice of Jesus. In other words, God sacrificed Himself to Himself.[35]

The issue of a restoration of a proper relationship between God and people is so critical and of such everlasting importance that it required a sacrifice that was worthy. Only God, who alone is worthy, can provide such a worthy sacrifice. Nothing else—no animal sacrifice; no sacrifice by a sinful, imperfect person is adequate. Only God Himself is able to provide a sacrifice that is worthy enough to be acceptable to Himself. The price of redemption was paid; the legal requirement was fulfilled by what Jesus did. Jesus's earthly life, death, and resurrection was the only worthy sacrifice of God, by God, and to God. To redeem us.

In Deborah's song, she talks about redemption, establishing the theological significance of the events of the battle by identifying patterns of redemption (Judges 5:4-7). Deborah's Song is similar to Stephen's speech at his stoning. It also points backward to Hannah's song (1 Samuel 2:1-20) and forward to Hebrews' recounting and elsewhere in Scripture which record how God delivered His people. God's redemption in the Old Testament was completed by His power. So was God's redemption in the New Testament—completed by His power in the work of Jesus. The implication is clear: the same God who delivered His people from Egypt is the same God who delivers His people today. We have confidence of that truth today, because Scripture reminds us that God is "the same yesterday and today and forever" (Hebrews 13:8).[36]

---

[35] Ibid.
[36] Duguid, *ESV Commentary*, 561.

Understanding and trusting in God's character and recognizing that He has included us in His plan of redemption is cause to sing. Deborah's song reminds us once more to trust in God's plan. That plan has been at work throughout history. When everything else in our lives feels like it is falling apart, in disarray and misery, God still stands. His plan continues and we remain securely part of that plan.

Who are we to God? When we recognize that we are part of God's plan of redemption and sing in praise, we understand how God might see His women of faith. We can respond:

"I am like Deborah."

For Thought and Discussion

- What specific fulfilled promise in Scripture gives you great confidence in God's character? How does that confidence encourage you today?

- What does redemption mean to you? How do you experience Christ's redemption?

I Sing of Redemption

- What Christian song—old hymn or contemporary song—helps you praise God for His redemption? Can you download the lyrics or music to sing that song? Or write your own song of praise?

PRAYER: Heavenly Father, thank you for redeeming me through what Christ did on the cross. Help me remember what that redemption means. Help me sing a song of redemption in my heart to praise you. Amen.

Day 28—I am like Deborah

☙❧

Of all the judges in Scripture, only Deborah's death is not recorded. Some Bible scholars believe this symbolically indicates that, she lives eternally and confirms the effectiveness of her rule. Moreover, Deborah left a lasting example of faith and leadership which has inspired future generations of people faithful to God. Our example of faith can inspire future generations also.

Over the last 27 days we have looked at the character and circumstances of Deborah. We have seen that Deborah spoke for God. We recognize that we, too must wait on God. We, too can speak God's Word. We, too can trust in God's plan. We, too can have fire in our eyes for Him. Our challenge is now:

What message do I sense God asking me to share with others? In what situation must I wait on God with full reliance and trust in Him?

We have also seen that we have a role in judgment, being wise and just, not judging other people's righteousness but remembering that we are accountable to God for what He asks us to do or not do. Our challenge is now:

> *What is God calling me to do? How has He equipped me for that work, not comparing myself to others but wholly focusing on His plan?*

We have also seen that we are called to be leaders. We recognize that leadership includes serving others, facing difficulties, providing inspiration, leading others and signaling others to follow God. Our challenge is now:

> *What leadership role does God intend for me personally and how can I serve others in that role to accomplish God's plan?*

We have also seen that we are called to be warrior women, standing courageously with faith in adversity, even amid overwhelming odds, supporting those who wield God's power, and empowering others. Our challenge is now:

> *In what area of my life am I battling evil? How can I unleash the power of the Holy Spirit in this situation and watch God's victory?*

We have also seen that we can live the meaning of the name Deborah, understanding the importance of unity of God's people, working hard and persevering in our faith, welcoming spiritual transformation, and producing spiritual fruit. Our challenge is now:

> *What spiritual gifts has God empowered me with and how can I use them to build up His church?*

I am Like Deborah

We have also seen that we can sing the Song of Deborah in our lives, seeing God's battle, recognizing His cosmic power, praising Him with thanksgiving, and singing of His redemption. Our challenge now is:

How can I remember what God has done, is doing, and will do each day so that my life is filled with thanksgiving and praise for including me in His plan?

There are many strong women whose lives are preserved in Scripture. Deborah is one of those women. She was a judge who led the nation of Israel. She was a prophetess who not only reminded the people of God's word, she actually spoke for Him to the people. Although not a military strategist, she also led the Israelite army to victory over their oppressive enemy, reminding her people—and us—of God's ultimate victory, His plan of redemption, and how He can use each of us to help accomplish that plan

There's another tidbit of information about the recording of Deborah's battle. Scripture tells us that she called Barak to gather the troops at Mt. Tabor. Mt. Tabor was about 12 miles north of the ancient city of Megiddo located on the plain or valley of Megiddo.[37] Other battles had occurred in that location (e.g., Joshua 12:21). King Solomon used the area for headquarters for his chariot and garrisons. Zechariah prophesied that the restoration for Israel and Jerusalem would occur on the plain of Megiddo (Zechariah 12:1).[38] In the book of Revelation, the final battle against evil will take place at the mound of *Har Megiddon*, translated as "Armageddon"

---

[37] Comfort, *Tynedale Bible Dictionary*, 877.
[38] Ibid.

I am Like Deborah

(Revelation 14:14-16). Megiddo is the physical, geographical place. Armageddon is its name as a symbolic location for God's ultimate battle where He is victorious over Satan completely and for all eternity.

This link between Deborah's battle against the evil forces of Sisera at Megiddo and God's ultimate battle against evil at Armageddon, remind us that the lessons we can learn from Deborah are eternal. God's plan is set out from Genesis, when God first declared war on Satan (Genesis 3:15) putting enmity between the woman and the serpent. The battles continue to be fought until God's ultimate victory described in the book of Revelation. Deborah's example and her lessons can teach us to stay on the path of faithfulness, just as she urged her people to do thousands of years ago.

With that thought, I further urge you to consider additional, more personal applications as you study the women in the Bible. The theme of this *With Faith Like Hers* series is that our lives, like theirs, are part of God's ongoing plan. As I was writing this series, my daughter suggested we honor these women in some unique, more personal way. Our business, Her Legacy Beauty[39] was born.

Our business creates beauty products in fragrances that honor biblical women to reflect their unique character or circumstances. Christian women appreciate the reminder of those women's lives in Scripture and find that wearing a unique fragrance is often a conversation starter to talk about Jesus. "Oh, you smell so good," your friend might say. You respond with, "Let me tell you about the woman whose fragrance I'm wearing and her place in the Bible." Your friend has just opened a conversation to talk about Jesus.

---

[39] www.HerLegacyBeauty.com.

This example is not about me peddling my company. This is about me encouraging you to find a way to incorporate your understanding of these women in the Bible into your daily life. Study the women. Consider how their character and circumstances are similar to your own. Then do something with that understanding. You might be surprised where it leads. I was.

As we continue to learn the lessons Deborah can teach us as women of faith today, the overriding theme she leaves us is that like Deborah, we can speak out on behalf of God—with wisdom, to fight evil, to pursue and speak God's plan.

One day we'll meet in Heaven and Jesus will call us by name. If He shouts out, "Deborah" will we all answer—since our character and circumstances are so like hers? That would probably make Jesus smile, knowing that we understand how He sees His women of faith. Until then,

Love, Deborah

I am Like Deborah

For Thought and Discussion

- In what ways did you not relate to Deborah at the beginning of this study?

- In what ways can you now relate to Deborah?

- Which lessons might you still need to work on from Deborah's character or circumstances?

PRAYER: Heavenly Father, thank you for the people whose lives you have recorded in Scripture. Please keep me learning lessons from their lives and show me how you desire to see me as one of your women of faith. Amen.

Resources

The following are a few of the resources used in preparation of this book. Each of the scholarly resources also have their own extensive bibliographies. If you want to dig deeper, you can work your way through those bibliographies.

Baker, Warren and Eugene Carpenter, eds. *Complete Word Study Dictionary Old Testament*. Chattanooga, TN: AMG, 2003.

Baker, Warren, DRE, Tim Rake, and David Kemp, eds. *Complete Word Study Old Testament, King James Version*. Chattanooga, TN: AMG, 1994.

> These two volumes work together as a single resource for Old Testament Hebrew words and phrases. When researching a specific word or phrase, first go to the *Old Testament* volume and find the specific word. Above that word will be a code. That code is then used to locate exactly how that original word in Hebrew was used—it's meaning and intention *in that specific verse of Scripture*. See the companion 2-volume set for the New Testament listed below.

Resources

Benner, Drayton, *ESV Exhaustive Concordance*. Wheaton, IL: Crossway. 2018.

> As its title describes, this concordance is "exhaustive." It lists passages according to specific words they contain. For example, taking the word "fear," this concordance then lists almost 400 verses that use that word (there are additional listings for "feared," fearful," "fearfully," "fearing," "fears" and "fearsome.") This resource can be helpful when researching specific topics.

Biblegateway.com.

> This is a fabulous online resource. It provides a quick and easy way to read the same Scripture in various versions for deeper understanding. It also has quite good commentaries that encourage a desire to find out more.

Buttrick, George Arthur, Commentary Editor. *Interpreter's Bible; The Holy Scriptures in the King James and Revised Standard Versions with General Articles and Introduction, Exegesis, Exposition for Each Book of the Bible, Vol. 2*. New York: Abingdon Press, 1952.

> This 12-volume Bible belonged to my Pastor dad who purchased them during or shortly after seminary. He used them for 45 years of sermon preparation. Now

they're my first go-to when I need solid, theological commentary or explanation. This important scholarly resource continues to be published, the latest edition as of the printing of this book was released by Abingdon Press in 2015.

Butterick, George A., *The Interpreter's Dictionary of the Bible, An Illustrated Encyclopedia.* New York: Abingdon Press, 1962.

This four-volume resource is valuable for understanding people and places discussed in the Bible. It includes archaeological discoveries as well as research into the life of people in ancient times.

Comfort, Philip W. and Walter A. Elwell, eds. *Tyndale Bible Dictionary.* Carol Stream: Tyndale, 2001.

This is an excellent resource to start researching individual words, phrases, and theological concepts.

Deen, Edith, *All of the Women of the Bible.* San Francisco: Harper San Francisco, 1983.

This book gives a general overview of women in Scripture. It is easy to read without being scholarly.

Duguid, Ian M., James M. Hamilton Jr., Jay Sklar, *ESV Expository Commentary, Vol II.* Crossway: Wheaton, IL, 2020.

Resources

This multi-volume resource is based on the English Standard Version (ESV) of the Bible. It contains both expository (explanation) and commentary (interpretation) which augments that of the *Interpreter's Bible* listed above.

Elwell, Walter A. and Robert W. Yarbrough, *Encountering the New Testament*. Grand Rapids: Baker Academic, 2013.

This is another seminary textbook. It is not, however, a resource that discusses verse-by-verse interpretations, such as in other commentary or expository sources. This is a more general overview of the books of the New Testament, with a degree of theological discussions and some treatment of thematic teachings of Jesus and Paul. This resource was helpful in viewing how the story of Deborah fit with the overall biblical theme extending from Genesis through Revelation.

Elwell, Walter A. *Baker Commentary on the Bible Based on the NIV*. Grand Rapids, MI: Baker Books, 1989.

This single-volume resource provides short and concise commentary on the entire Bible. Thus, it is a good first resource to get a handle on individual sections of Scripture that help get a person started on deeper research.

Elwell, Walter A. *Theological Dictionary*. Grand Rapids, MI: Baker Book House, 1989.

Resources

This resource and the one below are two different theological dictionaries. While there is some overlap, both are good resources to begin an understanding on words, phrases, and theological concepts.

Elwell, Walter A., ed., *Evangelical Dictionary of Theology*, Grand Rapids: Baker Academic, 2001.

Like the one above, this is another excellent resource to start research on individual words, phrases, and theological concepts.

Green, Jay. P, Sr., *The Interlinear Bible Hebrew-Greek-English*. Peabody, MS: Hendrickson Publishers. 1986.

This is a single volume of the Bible with each word of text containing the Hebrew or Greek word used in the original. Each word is tied to the Strong's Concordance number for cross-referencing. This, like the Baker and Zodhiates resources, help better interpret Scripture in a word-by-word format.

Hamilton, Victor P., *Handbook on the Historical Books: Joshua, Judges, Ruth, Samuel, Kings Chronicles, Ezra-Nehemiah, Esther*. Grand Rapids, MI: Baker Academic, 2001.

This seminary textbook conducts an in-depth exegesis (biblical study) of the historical books in the Old Testament. Of specific help was the section on Judges, but also the books of the Bible prior to and after to understand the pattern of God's allowing the Israelites to fall away from Him and then allowing oppression

Resources

from neighboring nations followed by His redemption to return them to faith.

OpenBible.info

This is another good online resource with an ability to search based on a word or topic. Although the results sometimes feel computer generated (because they are!) it's still a good place to start expanding a line of thinking.

New Strong's Concise Concordance of the Bible. Nashville: Thomas Nelson, 2005.

This resource is helpful to understand meaning of original words in Scripture and locating passages.

Vine, W.E., Merrill F. Unger, William White, Jr., *Vine's Complete Expository Dictionary of Old and New Testament Words.* Nashville: Thomas Nelson Publishers, 1996.

This Bible dictionary is helpful in understanding the meaning of the original words in Scripture.

Resources

Zondervan NIV Study Bible. Grand Rapids: Zondervan, 2002.

> This provides basic study notes for a quick overview of Scripture.

Zodhiates, Spiros, Warren Baker, George Hadjiantoniou, and Mark Oshman, eds. *Complete Word Study Dictionary New Testament.* Chattanooga: AMG, 1993.

Zodhiates, Spiros, Warren Baker, and George Hadjiantoniou, *Complete Word Study Old Testament, King James Version.* Chattanooga: AMG, 1992.

> These two volumes work together as a single resource for New Testament Greek words and phrases. When researching a specific word or phrase, first go to the *New Testament* volume and find the specific word. Above that word will be a code. That code is then used to locate exactly how that original word in Hebrew was used—it's meaning and intention *in that specific verse of Scripture.* See the companion 2-volume set for the Old Testament listed above.

The best and most valuable source always—is prayer, study, and God's leading. It's easy and tempting to come up with personal theology and proclaim it brilliant. It's harder, but always best, to rely on God's leading and to check any "personal brilliance" against the truth of God's Word set forth in Scripture.

From the Author

I was raised in a Christian home. But it wasn't until I was in my late twenties that I took full ownership of my faith and began the long process of learning what it means to be a Christian and a child of God. I'm still learning.

When I began writing, I was blessed by early publishing success when my first four books were picked up by a respected children's educational publisher. My mission became to write in a way that would educate, inspire, and entertain others.

Gradually I moved from writing for children to writing for women seeking to deepen their faith. Someone once said that "all writing is basically autobiographical." That's true for me. As I write this Bible study series. I seek to understand and deepen my own faith as I write to help other women understand and deepen theirs.

I live in Idaho with my husband of almost 50 years. I have two grown children and two grandsons, all of whom taught me that if God only loves me a fraction of how much I love them—wow, God loves me a lot!

This book is part of a series of Bible studies/Daily Devotionals about women of the Bible. To find other books in this series, please go to Amazon.com. Search for the series by typing *With Faith Like Hers* followed by *I am*. Each title will begin with "I am" followed by the name of that woman.

If you enjoyed this study, please let others know. One of the best ways to let folks know is to leave a review. Just go to Amazon.com, find the title of this book and click on "Write a Customer Review." Thanks in advance!